# FULFILLING YOUR POTENTIAL

Discover, Develop & Deploy Your Talents

**SOLOMON OSOKO**

# FULFILLING YOUR POTENTIAL:

## Discovering, Developing & Deploying Your Talents

Copyright © 2019 by Solomon Osoko
All rights reserved.

The copyright laws of Switzerland protect this book.
No portion of this book may be copied or reprinted for commercial gain without the written permission of the author and publisher, except brief excerpts in articles, magazines or reviews.
The use of short quotation and occasional copying for personal or group study is permitted and encouraged.
Unless otherwise identified, all scripture quotations are from the King James Version of the Bible.

ISBN -13: 978-3-9524512-5-0
**Published in Switzerland.**

For further information, contact:

**Solomon Osoko Ministries**
www.solomonosoko.com
sales@solomonosoko.com

**Solomon Osoko**

# DEDICATION

I dedicate this book to my siblings:

**ACP Olubunmi Osoko**

**Adedayo Osoko**

**Afolake Akinbowale (Nee Osoko)**

**Pastor Sola Osoko**

**Kunmi Osoko**

We came into the world as brothers and sister
We walk together not separating from one another
Being brothers and sister means being there for each other

CONTENTS

FORWARD: DESTINY RELOADED ............................................5
INTRODUCTION: RUNNING WITH FULL POTENTIAL......11
CHAPTER 1: WHAT IS POTENTIAL? ......................................15
CHAPTER 2: THE PRINCIPLES OF POTENTIAL ...................25
CHAPTER 3: THE ENEMIES OF POTENTIAL........................38
CHAPTER 4: DISCOVERING YOUR POTENTIAL ................50
CHAPTER 5: THE POWER OF POTENTIAL ..........................66
CHAPTER 6: RELEASING YOUR POTENTIAL.......................75
CHAPTER 7: DEVELOPING YOUR POTENTIAL...................90
CHAPTER 8: THE PLACE OF LABOUR ................................103
CHAPTER 9: DEPLOYING YOUR POTENTIAL ...................111
CHAPTER 10: PROTECTING YOUR POTENTIAL................121
CHAPTER 11: EXERCISING DOMINION MANDATE .........130
CHAPTER 12: ENVIRONMENTAL STEWARDSHIP.............143
CHAPTER 13: BECOMING A PERSON OF VALUE .............151
CHAPTER 14: BLESSED BY CHOICE ...................................168

# FORWARD: DESTINY RELOADED

*And God said, Let us make man in our image, after our likeness: and let them have dominion over the fish of the sea, and over the fowl of the air, and over the cattle, and over all the earth, and over every creeping thing that creepeth upon the earth.* $^{27}$ *So God created man in his image, in the image of God created he him; male and female created he them.* $^{28}$ *And God blessed them, and God said unto them, Be fruitful, and multiply, and replenish the earth, and subdue it: and have dominion over the fish of the sea, and over the fowl of the air, and over every living thing that moveth upon the earth.* **Gen. 1:26-28**

Everyman is born with the potential to live a fruitful existence. What is mostly lacking is the ability to let it out.
Though potential is infinite, everyone is limited by the limits one puts on self. The key to fulfilling your life purpose, is in discovering, developing and deploying your potential.
Like a seed, your fruits are lying dormant within you.
The same way a seed carries everything necessary to become the tree it is meant to become, so does every creature carries all the potential necessary to fulfill destiny and purpose on earth. The same way a maize farm is packaged inside a handful of corn seeds is your greatness and future wrapped inside of your potential, waiting to be let out.
You are a seed that has been blessed to be fruitful.
Being great can be as simple as becoming yourself.
A seed of mango is created to bear mango fruits not orange.
Many people are frustrated in life because they failed to take note of their potential as a pointer to their ordained destiny. They waste time copying, envying and wanting to be like other people. What a wrong pursuits!

## Stop waste!
The primary way people are tricked by the enemy to lose value in life is to lose view of their potential and waste time in the pursuits of other things. Many are the plans in the mind of a man, but it is the purpose of the Lord that will stand (Prov.19:21)!
God knows that your greatness is only located in you becoming you. Another attack of the enemy could be in uprooting you from your right environment. Seek to be cultivated in the right environment that brings out the best in you. Your environment includes the people around you. He who walks with the wise will become wise, but the companion of fools will be destroyed (Prov.13:20.)

As a seed needs the right environment, so do you.
Once you are rooted, with a steadfast commitment to growth and resolve to endure all the seasons of life till your season to bear fruits come, it is a matter of time for you to fulfil your life's purpose.
All you need to do is pursue with persistence your goals to the end.
Do not be afraid of the unknown terrain ahead of you.
You carry great potential within you.
You are created to be a god on earth – for you are created in the image of God (your Heavenly Father.)
You share God's attributes which are great potentials for creativity.
Imagine, God created the whole world from nothing.
Yes, you and I are meant to create our world from God's deposits in us.
We have enormous deposits of potential in us to create too.
We just need the creativity to see the opportunity in every situation.
There is always potential in you and in your situation or environment to create your desired goal only if you exercise your endless creativity.
Whenever you go through any stubborn situation, be reminded that you are wired to be fruitful, to multiply, to replenish, subdue and have dominion on earth (Genesis 1.26-28).
Do not be discouraged by your present situation.
Potential is all that you can become that you are yet to become.
God, from the onset, never gave man complete products to accomplish his dominion mandate on earth. Everything man would ever need is however deposited in him as a potential - left at the mercy of his creativity. Adam did not drive in cars; neither did the people in the time of Jesus Christ flew in airplanes because their creativity and knowledge of technology then could not process the ever available steel.
They could not enjoy electricity or watch television programs because their intellects were not developed enough to create the modern day technology that we now enjoy. Now we have enough creativity and technology to enjoy much more in life.
Why will you chose to live below the potential of the day, for instance and chose to power your business with coal instead of electricity?
Yet many people carry what is greater and mightier than electricity within but chose to live a life of weakness and irrelevance.
Every man carries unlimited potentials to live a distinguished life in different fields regardless of any situation.
Mediocrity is living below your potential.

It is enough of living a mediocre life dictated by fear, unbelief and insecurity. Why will you live so secured as if the aim of life is to survive? The irony of it all is that no one ever survived this life alive!
You are not created to hide your potential.
You are instead created to develop, release, and use it.
The greatest tragedy of life is not in dying young but in living long without discovering or fulfilling your potential.
You are created so you can use potential and die empty.
Jesus Christ lived for 33 years, and the impact of His short sojourn on earth is still affecting the entire humanity till now.
If you live, unaware of your potential, you cannot achieve your destiny nor fulfil God's purpose for your life.
You need to discover your potential to achieve your destiny.
You need to achieve your destiny to fulfil God's purpose for your life.
Ignorance of your potential is, therefore, a sure guarantee for an undiscovered destiny and unfulfilled purpose.
Potential discovered is destiny reloaded.
It is time to reload your destiny.
It is time to celebrate your uniqueness because there is only one of you.

> You are God's type,
> possessing the unlimited potential for creativity.
> You are a bundle of potential.
> You can be more. You can do more.

## Your potential has the answer to your comeback

We sometimes fail in life, and that is human and natural.
What is not good is to permit your temporary situation to define your personality. No one should allow past failure to define the present or defile the future. You always have the potential to come back and rise. That is why the Bible says that even when a righteous man falls seven times, he can still rise. Whatever failure, pain or loss you may have suffered in the past, the answer to your recovery, survival and restoration remains in your potential. History is filled with stories of men who have used their setbacks as a launchpad for their comeback.

- **Henry Ford**, before he made a name in the automotive industry, made some wrong business steps and had to file for bankruptcy twice. He finally succeeded in creating a motor vehicle he could be proud of and that the world came to respect and patronise. That breakthrough sustained him and his beneficiaries in the realm of wealth.
- **Walt Disney**, faced with mounting debts and no money to pay his bills, filed bankruptcy in 1923. The same year he formed a new film company using a loan from his parents and brother. With his debts forgiven and his new company properly financed, in 1928 Disney created his most iconic character-Mickey Mouse. Nearly ten years after that he released Snow White and the Seven Dwarfs, and the rest is history. Those films and many other creations of Disney gave him extraordinary success in his career.
- **Oprah Winfrey** was sexually abused at the age of 9 yet grew up to be one of the most influential women in the World. Pastor **Joyce Meyer** was equally abused by her father until she left home at the age of eighteen. These two ladies did not permit their past to decide their future, yet rose up to become leading figures in their careers. They did not allow past pains to deprive them of life gains.
- **Bill Gate** dropped out of university to pursue his passion for Information Technology. At once in history, he became the richest man on earth. Contrary to what people think, mastering some information in school is no recipe for success. School is only meant to polish the potentials God already deposited in you at birth. You can make it to the top of your career ladder with your potentials, with or without any formal education.
- **Steve Jobs** shared the same experience with his colleague and business partner, Bill Gates. Growing up, Steve Jobs had a hard time with formal schooling (due to boredom), so he dropped out of college to pursue his creative and innovative career in Information Technology. He became an inventor, designer and entrepreneur. Jobs co-founded Apple at the age of 21 and were worth millions by age 23. Then he was fired from his own company. That was devastating enough to break down many people but not Steve (who claimed in a 2005 interview that getting fired from Apple was the best thing that could have ever happened to him). Steve Jobs started his second company, NeXT, which was ultimately acquired by Apple--and Jobs became CEO again. He later created iPad, iTunes, iMac and other very successful Apple

products. Steve Jobs died a multi-billionaire in Palo Alto on October 5, 2011, after battling pancreatic cancer for nearly a decade.
- **Harland Sanders**, the founder of KFC, was on the verge of suicide when an idea struck him to use his mum's old family recipe to prepare chicken for sales. The rest is history. KFC has become an international franchise earning business that continues to win the estate of Sanders fortune many years after his demise. His life experience teaches that past failures are no threats to greatness.
- **Tony Blair**, the former British Prime Minister, narrated that he was called a failure by his teachers, but he rose up and became a Prime Minister of the United Kingdom. His experience teaches that you should refuse to believe any opinion of people that is contrary to your personal belief and conviction. Just believe in your potential!
- **Nelson Mandela** was in prison for 27 years and still became president of South Africa. During incarceration, he refused to give up his hope to lead his country and kept fanning the fire of potentials inside of him. He continued to develop his leadership potential even in prison. That step did not only protect him from the Apartheid government's sponsored murder but aided him to become the first African president to lead the democratic nation of South Africa. His experience proved that it is never too late to fulfil your dream. Don't let your past decide the kind of future you need to have.
- **Barack Hussein Obama** as the son of a black immigrant from Kenya faced a lot of challenges in the United States of America, but he never allowed them to hinder him. He struggled through Harvard University to train as a lawyer and then joined politics. He climbed up the political ladder from being a grassroot organizer to become the first black African President of the United States of America.

In all these stories, something stands very clear.
The discovery of potential leads to the recovery of destiny!
The source of a comeback from any setback is in the potential you carry.
Each of these great persons recovered by falling back on potentials.
Only those who will attempt to go far will know how far one can go.
Nothing can stop a person who has made up his mind to move forward.
Trust in the Lord and have faith in the potential He has put in you.
You have all it takes to prevail over all trials and tribulations that may ever come your way. You are too loaded to fail.

*No temptation has overtaken you except what is common to mankind. And God is faithful; he will not let you be tempted beyond what you can bear. But when you are tempted, he will also provide a way out so that you can endure it. 1 Cor.10:13*

All you need to get back is to have faith in God and to believe in yourself. The Bible teaches that all things are possible to him that believes.
When God permits trials to pull you down, it is not to bury you, but to plant you. When God permits you to be thrown in the fire, it is not to burn you but to refine you. When God allows you to pass through the waters, it is not to drown you, but to cleanse you.
Joseph was planted in a pit and grew up to become a prime minister in a foreign nation. The three Hebrew boys were thrown into the furnace of fire and came out as refined governors of the foreign land. Naaman thought he was ridiculed to be asked to swim in Jordan river seven times but came out at the other side completely cleansed from leprosy.
You have the potential to recover from every fall if only you will decide to rise. The potential inside you will rise and give you all you need to prevail. If you believe you can make it, yes you can!

## It is time for your destiny to be reloaded!
Yes, you can still break out of a life of mediocrity into that of excellence. Choose to break free of social, cultural and physical limits.
Stop judging your life by your past failure or present accomplishment.
He that is in you is greater than he that is in the world.
You are God's type, possessing the unlimited potential for creativity.
You are a bundle of potential. You can be more. You can do more.
Your gifts and capabilities have no limits.
You can do all things through Jesus Christ that strengthens you!
This book has come to ignite your life with that fire that you need to fulfil your potential. It is written specifically to help you discover, develop and deploy your potential so that you can fulfil your destiny and accomplish God's purpose for your life.
Let me accompany you on your journey of fulfilment with this book.
Tighten your seat belt for a life-transforming voyage and get ready to say a resolute goodbye to a life of mediocrity.
It is a new day, and your journey of exploits has just begun.

## INTRODUCTION: RUNNING WITH FULL POTENTIAL

*Wherefore seeing we also are compassed about with so great a cloud of witnesses, let us lay aside every weight, and the sin which doth so easily beset us, and let us run with patience the race that is set before us.* **Heb.12:1**

Life is a spiritual race.
You are here on earth on purpose and your clock is already ticking on. If you miss that point, you may waste your entire existence in pursuit of vain goals and glory.
It is just too easy to copy any of the billions of great creatures walking all around you. Stop running another man's race!
Many people have lost focus of their life. They have lost the sight of their destiny and purpose - the only ticket to the comity of stars.
You are destined to be you. The world is filled with people running all types of rat race that is leading to nowhere.

## 1. ARE YOU RUNNING YOUR RACE?

*"We are not human beings having a spiritual experience. We are spiritual beings having a human experience"* – Pierre Teilhard de Chardin

Your spiritual race has given you a part to play in God's purpose for humanity across several nations and generations. He is the Lord of all flesh and all ages, and regardless of the individual destiny, everyman has a role to play in God's purpose for the entire humankind.
Individual destiny is meant to prepare all of us for God's purpose.
No matter how our destinies may be, we are all expected to make the best use of His grace upon our lives.
Be careful that you are running God's race for your life and not a race you set for your life or the one that other people plan for you.
Those are rat races that make a man live in frustration rather than in fulfilment. God and the hosts of heaven are not interested in our carnal races. They are only interested in our spiritual race.
Only those who focus on running their God-appointed race can maximise life on earth to finish the race (2 Timothy 4:7.)
Only such can fulfil God's purpose for their lives.
That is why divine direction would remain a priceless asset in running the race of your life to completion. Nothing is as important as running the race of your life according to God's instruction and direction.
It makes the race faster, easier and more enjoyable.

## 2. ARE YOU RUNNING WITH YOUR FULL POTENTIAL?

*I praise you because I am fearfully and wonderfully made; your works are wonderful, I know that full well* **Psalm 139:14 (NIV)**

It's a question that comes to all of us from time to time.
This book aims to help you answer that question and many more.
Be warned, however, that this book intends to take you out of your comfort zone and lead you on a daring journey of self-manifestation that only self-discovery can guide you. The good news is that with the knowledge of who God is and who you are in Him, becoming who He created you to be can be both fulfilling and challenging.
The good news is that the Holy Trinity had a consultation concerning you before you were ever formed. Your existence was setup for success because you have a destiny and purpose to fulfil on earth.

## 3. ON YOUR MARK, GET READY

*Therefore, since we are surrounded by so great a cloud of [a]witnesses [who by faith have testified to the truth of God's absolute faithfulness] stripping off every unnecessary weight and the sin which so easily and cleverly entangles us, let us run with endurance and active persistence the race that set before us.* **Heb.12:1**

What will you do if you know that your vision cannot fail?
Like every manufacturer, God creates you for success.
Your fulfilment is guaranteed because your earthly existence has the backing of God the Father, God the Son and God the Holy Ghost.
Prepare to run the race, therefore to the very end with confidence.
You need to run your race with persistence and patience (Hebrews 12:1).
To run this spiritual race successfully, you also need to lay aside every weight and sin which clings so tightly and run with endurance the race that is set before you. If you fail to prepare, you prepare to fail.
As you prepare yourself to run the race of your life with adequate preparation and discipline, your race can only end in excellence.

### Rules for running successfully

**a) Run your race (Heb.12:1)**
Many Christians are misguided by wrong church doctrines to run after wealth, materialism, fame and the pursuits of other selfish temporal ambition rather than running foremost after the kingdom of God.

God's instruction is clear, "But seek first the kingdom of God and His righteousness, and all these things will be added to you (Matt 6:33)". Disobedience to this straightforward instruction has left many Christians disoriented, worried, stressed and sometimes suicidal as they run after every other thing, hoping the kingdom of God and its blessing would be added to them. While pursuits of mundane things like work, wealth and good health are essential, they should not be pursued at the expense of our spiritual priority of seeking God. Without honoring God foremost, the pursuits of temporary earthly blessings could only lead to greed, selfishness, depression and other forms of destruction. Christian's race is not about the greedy acquisition of material and temporal things and other rat race of life. Jesus warned us that we must watch out and be on guard against all kinds of greed for, "life does not consist in an abundance of possessions (Luke 12:15)." Run the race set for you!

b) **Run your race according to your unique ability (Heb.12:1)**
The same way David refused to wear Saul's armour before battling Goliath, do we need to cast aside the armour of other warriors if we are to win our battles. Throw off everything that hinders and all sins that so easily entangles. You need to utilise the capacity God has given you in the pursuits of your assignments.

c) **Run according to the rules of the game (2 Tim.2:5)**
You need to run the race for your lives according to God's plan, purpose and principles. The same way it is in the natural race that those who do not run according to rules can be disqualified, can we also be disqualified if we run our God-given race without observing God's rules.

d) **Run according to God's timing (Eccl 3:1)**
There is a time and a season for all God's purpose. Many people miss God's sure reward because it always comes at the end. To God's purpose, there is a time (Hab. 2:3.) Moses ran faster than his time and delayed God's purpose for an additional thirty years. That is why mastering endurance is a great skill for reaching the end of your race.

e) **Run with focus (1 Cor. 9:24-26)**
You need to stay focused to fulfil your calling.
Living purposefully helps to organise your life and order your pursuits. Broken focus is the primary reason why many people fail.
As long as Peter kept his sight on Jesus Christ, he was able to walk on water. Sometimes, all it takes to lose our race in life is to allow our pains and disappointments to distract us from focussing on the Lord.

Permit no sin or business to break your focus from Jesus Christ, the Author and Finisher of your faith in the pursuits of your life mission. Learn to focus and be committed to what matters most.

### f) Run with discipline (1 Cor. 9:27)

Life race is a marathon rather than a sprint, so discipline is required.
You need to run with perseverance the race marked out for us.
Victory in any race is always declared at the end.
Every athlete needs self-discipline and stamina to run the race to the end.
Even though the vision of your race delays, wait [patiently] for it, because it will certainly come; it will not delay.

### g) Run to win

People cheer you as you run your race with strength, focus and the determination not to loose. Prepare to run till the end.
You are imbued with great potential for an excellent existence!
All that is required to reveal the excellence buried in you is a process of self-awareness, self-development and self- manifestation.
People don't appreciate you because you are kind and cool.
You have to appreciate for people to appreciate you.
They appreciate you because you have appreciated in what they value.
They appreciate you because you do not give up.
You are not celebrated for starting a thing but for perfecting and finishing it. Winners are finishers. Run to the end. Run to win.

## 4. GO!

*Ask and it will be given to you; seek and you will find; knock and the door will be opened to you. Matt. 7:7*

Never confuse means of living with what you are living for!
We are not just on earth to pay our bills, feed and die.
The purpose of our existence is to add values to humanity?
Running your race is about consciously taking a step forward, one at a time, in pursuits of your life assignment.
If you don't pursue your purpose on earth, you will never attain it.
If you don't ask, you shall not be given. If you do not seek, you may not find. If you refuse to knock the door, it may not be opened for you.
Until you step forward, you will remain in the same spot.

You have all it takes to become whom God purposed you to be!
It remains, however, your responsibility to release the inherent potential you are endowed with to fulfil your unique purpose. That process begins with self-awareness.
You need to know who you are and the talents you carry!

**Solomon Osoko**

# SECTION 1:

# DISCOVERING YOUR POTENTIAL (SELF-AWARENESS)

*We now have this light shining in our hearts, but we ourselves are like fragile clay jars containing this great treasure. This makes it clear that our great power is from God, not from ourselves.* ***2 Cor. 4:7***

# CHAPTER 1: WHAT IS POTENTIAL?

*We now have this light shining in our hearts, but we ourselves are like fragile clay jars containing this great treasure. This makes it clear that our great power is from God, not from ourselves.* **2 Cor.4:7**

There is a great future and a vital purpose ahead of everyman. That is because every man has the potential, that is the necessary abilities or qualities to become self and achieve life purpose.
You are wholly wired to be you.
You have all it takes to become whom God purposed you to be!
It remains, however, your responsibility to release the inherent potential you are endowed with to fulfil your unique purpose.
That process begins with self-awareness.
You need to know who you are and the talents you carry!
For instance, hidden inside a baby is a woman or a man.
All that the baby needs to do is to complete the process of growth.
God hides great things in small things called potential.
Growth process entails developing your capacity from what it is to what it should be.
On a personal scale, every man is packaged with a heavenly solution for human needs. However like it is with onion, until you pull out one layer, you cannot access the next. There is a lot to your life than you see.
Self-actualisation is a process of developing, maturing and growing up – one step at a time.

a) **Potential is the Maker's deposits in its product to achieve the purpose of its existence.**

*We now have this light shining in our hearts, but we ourselves are like fragile clay jars containing this great treasure.* **2 Cor. 4:7a**

Potential is an unlimited resource of God in all His creation.
Potential is all you can become that you are yet to become
Every manufacturer prepares a product for a purpose and builds in it, the potential to make that product fulfil its purpose. Every assignment also demands unique potential that God has given into individuals

### b) Potential can be described as a hidden glory

*But we ourselves are like fragile clay jars containing this great treasure. 2 Cor. 4:7a*

It is a guarantee for a colourful and glorious existence for every man.
God hid greatness in the clay of jar called a man so that all the credits for human greatness can be traced to God. This way, every time a person fulfils his purpose, God the Creator is glorified. In the best of time, many of us are like broken down jars that the power of God puts together and shines through. As people see us, they take notice of the light of God shining through our scars and broken parts.

### c) Potential is the idea of the omnipotent God to share His glory with His creatures.

*This makes it clear that our great power is from God, not from ourselves. 2 Cor.4:7b*

Potential is God's idea of granting His creatures' relevance and fulfilment. Our great power is not from us but is from God!
Potential is just divine insurance for a colourful and glorious existence for every man.

### d) It is a hidden ability to make you live in excellence

*And we know that all things work together for good to them that love God, to them who are the called according to his purpose. Rom. 8:28*

It is the divine stamp of authority to ascend your throne on earth.
Potential is God's idea of granting His creatures' relevance and fulfilment.
It is your secret code to access your realm of appreciation and relevance.
So long you stay connected to your Maker's plan and purpose for your life, diligently serving the potential deposited in you, all things shall work out together for your good.
Potential is the light of God hidden in every believer that God expects to be revealed so that the world can know Him through us.

### e) It is God's hidden power in every regenerated man

*Now unto Him that is able to do exceeding abundantly above all that we ask or think, according to the power that worketh in us. Eph. 3:20.*

Potential is dormant, latent, passive and inactive power

Your potential is the hidden resources, abilities and capabilities deposited in every creature at birth. It is the inherent ability or capacity for great strength and power. It is a latent capacity to generate exceeding power. And God said, Let us make man in our image, after our likeness: and let them have dominion. So God created humanity in His image, in the image of God he created them; male and female he created them. (Gen. 1:26-27). The power of your life is not in your strength or accomplishment but in the grace of God ever made available for all your needs. The best you can achieve with your common knowledge is common sense and achievement. It takes the grace of God to do the extraordinary and supernatural. That was what Apostle Paul found out when God told him, " My grace is sufficient for you, for my power is made perfect in weakness." Therefore I will boast all the more gladly about my weaknesses, so that Christ's power may rest on me ( 2 Cor.12:9). God said the same to Zerubbabel saying, 'Not by might nor by power, but by My Spirit,' says the LORD of hosts (Zech.4:6). The claim of Zerubbabel to victory was to be grace not personal might. Grace is God's power.

### f) Potential is an unending source of power hidden in you

*Ye are of God, little children, and have overcome them: because greater is he that is in you, than he that is in the world. 1 John 4:4*

It is what makes a potent man while alive. It is the source of regular supply of strength and motivation to get your life assignment fulfilled. You see, you are like a cat with seven lives. You are armed with the divine potential to turn all your setbacks to setup for a great comeback. For though the righteous fall seven times, they rise again (Prov.24:16.) Potential is the powerful capacity of everyone dwelling in God. Stop being scared by the giants and the mountains in front of you. Greater is the one in you than the one in the world (1 John 4:4)!

### g) Potential is greatness hidden deep inside

*The kingdom of heaven is like unto a grain of mustard seed. Matt 13:31*

Potential refers to an unused ability, hidden gifts and untapped talents Just like a seed, all you need to become who you are created to be is already deposited inside you before you were born.

Inside the fetus is a hidden baby and inside every baby is a boy or a girl. Inside that boy and girl are a man and a woman. And as they continue to explore the potential inside together, they can become a family, source of families and then a big nation.

You see, man is fearfully and wonderfully created (Jer.1:5; Ps 139:14.)

You have the mind of Christ, the mind that created heaven and earth and all creations therein. All you need to break stagnation is to secure the vision for future. 1 Cor. 2:16; John 3:31

You are progressing today according to the level of your self-discovery. Potential is like a mustard seed that when one sows it, it is little but when it grows up, it houses multiple birds of the air.

### h) Potential is how far you can go with God

*"I said, 'You are "gods"; you are all sons of the Most High. 7 But you will die like mere mortals; you will fall like every other ruler."* **Psalm 82: 6-7**

*If he called them gods, to whom the word of God came, and the scripture cannot be broken.* **John 10:35**

Bible teaches that every son of God has a latent capacity to demonstrate a likeness of God. This is a biblical truth and not heresy or blasphemy. Jesus insisted that our status as gods is a scripture that can not be broken! He said in another place, that "I tell you the truth, anyone who believes in me will do the same works I have done, and even greater works, because I am going to be with the Father (John 14:12)."

### i) Potential is a pointer to life's purpose

Potential is a pointer to your design and destiny.
Knowing your potential helps you to discover your life purpose.
A baby girl is born with the potential to become a mother.
A boy has no potential to be pregnant so no matter how long he tries, it will be in vain. It is like trying to fly with a bicycle that has no potential to fly! On the contrary, every baby eagle has inbuilt potential to fly.
All it needs to do is develop the capacity through the growth process.

## The story of the talents

*For the kingdom of heaven is as a man travelling into a far country, who called his own servants, and delivered unto them his goods. 15 And unto one he gave five talents, to another two, and to another one; to every man according to his several ability; and straightway took his journey. 16 Then he that had received the five talents went and traded with the same, and made them other five talents. 17 And likewise he that had received two, he also gained other two. 18 But he that had received one went and digged in the earth, and hid his lord's money.* **Matt.25:14-18**

The story of talents is about a man entrusting his possessions to his servants according to their several abilities. To one he gave five talents, to another he gave two, and to the third, he gave one.
There is a similar parable in Luke 19:11-27 teaching the same concepts. When the master returned, the first two servants declared profits on their master's money and were commended as "good and faithful servants", while the third, claiming his master was a wicked man reported no profit for he had chosen to bury his talents. The unproductive servant was busy judging the master while he failed to take the responsibility to develop his talent – which was a measure of gold.
I wonder what this man with one talent was doing while the talent was buried. He was still able to maintain his life till the return of the Master. I guess he was employed to develop someone else's talent.
That is what employment does mostly. It prevents us from deployment. While employment is good for us all at a point in time as a means to learn to serve and develop our capacities, it is not meant to be the end of our life journey. It is only meant to prepare and provide for us until we can deploy our God-given talents and gifts.
There are lots of lessons one can learn from this story.
Foremost, there are different types of stewards and each one of us fits in to a type depending on how we handle the gifts God has given us.

## Which type of person are you?
The story of the talents teaches that there are three types of people:
- The minimum managers (who ignore their potential)
- The medium managers (who put potential to moderate use) and
- The extraordinary managers (who put potential to excellent use)

### a)    Minimum Managers (Lazy People)
This group refers to the people who completely ignore their God-given potential and talents through ignorance, lack of interest or sheer laziness.

They just left their potential buried, untapped, unreleased and wasted. Such never discover who they are or what their purpose in life is. They are simple people using their common sense and the minimal idea of their self- awareness to survive their everyday life. This group enjoys a basic existence. The minimum people bury their talents and blame everyone for their problems. They refuse to take responsibility for life.

b) **Medium Managers (Mediocre People)**

This group refers to the people that are barely living average or above average life. This group puts its potential to minimal development and use. Such people do not commit to excellent standards, so they are not especially distinguished.

While the good news is that such people can use their gifts and skills minimally to project a part of who they are, the sad news is that they could have achieved far more if only they will aspire to do so. The medium people are aware of their potential, and they develop it to an average extent where it provides for their existence. These people, however, are content with surviving and living a mediocre life.

c) **Maximum Managers ( Extra-ordinary people)**

The people in this group are committed to developing and maximizing their talents and gifts. They hone such to excellent skills that they use to add values to their lives and those of others connected to them.
The people in this group have distinguished themselves in their fields and offer superior service and conducts to the other two groups.
This third type of people explores their potential to the full.
They are the ones not content with the success of yesterday, and neither can any failure or challenge hinder them. They keep striving towards perfection knowing God's plan is to take them from glory to glory

---

Potential is a pointer to life's purpose
It is a pointer to your design and destiny.
Knowing your potential helps you to discover your life purpose.
A baby girl is born with the potential to become a mother.
A boy has no potential to be pregnant so
no matter how long he tries, it will be in vain.

---

## What type of manager are you?

*Moreover it is required in stewards, that a man be found faithful. 1 Cor.4:2*

The fact of life remains that whatever you have, you are given by God. The way you manage it determines the type of manager that you are. Everything on earth including you and all you have belongs to the Lord. You are just a steward, a manager that is expected to handle God's property faithfully. The question is, which type of steward are you?

**Talents and Management**

*The earth is the Lord's, and the fulness thereof; the world, and they that dwell therein. Psalm 24:1*

Talents are test of management skills!
With the talents God has blessed you with; He will test your management ability to determine the continuity of your rewards and blessing.
One man who demonstrated wise management of potentials in the Bible was Joseph. Though faced by much opposition, his management skill earned him the blessing of God and took him to the top of his carrier. Though a slave, Joseph's management skill made him the head of the household of Potiphar. Everything was left in his hands by Potiphar. Even when Potiphar falsely imprisoned, his skill still gave him a position of management over other prisoners. That skill soon brought him in contact with palace prisoners, one of which introduced him to the king for the translation of his dream. The king, Pharaoh, recognizing Joseph's management skill made him a high-level manager that was responsible for manage the affairs of Egypt as the land journeyed from prosperity into famine seasons.
God honours responsible stewards. He blesses mankind with salvation and honours our ability to manage the grace He grants us.
How good is your management ability?
Effective management of resources is a divine means of promotion. Joseph took God very seriously. He knew God was watching him at all time and that God was with him. Joseph managed himself well in prison and was promoted to serve in the palace.
God is still rewarding honest and diligent managers.

How great and excellent we will work if we know that God is watching us too. God is still waiting for people to promote.

*For the eyes of the LORD run to and fro throughout the whole earth, to shew himself strong in the behalf of them whose heart is perfect toward him. 2 Chr.16:9a*

*He that is faithful in that which is least is faithful also in much: and he that is unjust in the least is unjust also in much. 11 If therefore ye have not been faithful in the unrighteous mammon, who will commit to your trust the true riches? 12 And if ye have not been faithful in that which is another man's, who shall give you that which is your own? Luke 16:10-12*

The Bible teaches the importance of being honest in every little thing.
How faithful are you in the management of your potentials?
God will mostly promote you in life by blessing your management ability.
How faithful are you in the management of another man's things?
That will determine the extent God can bless you.
How faithful are you in labouring at your place of work?
A faithful manager of job uses his time to add values to the business. God, in turn, honours faithful labourers by pouring favour upon their labours. Well done you good and faithful labourer!
How faithful are you in handling your relationship with other people.
A man who has friends must show himself to be friendly (Prov.18:24).
A faithful manager of relationship does not abuse or misuse people.
Such add rich experience to other people's lives.
The extent you are faithful in the management of your finance will, for instance, determine how far you can be blessed. God once explained why some people are going through financial problems. He claimed it was because they were bad managers of His money. They have chosen to rob Him by not paying their tithes and offerings. He promised to open doors of heaven and blesses them if they will faithfully return to pay the tithes and offerings. What many believers do not realise is that tithing, like talents and other blessings from God, is a test in the management of God's resources. No wonder the Lord said, "Bring ye all the tithes into the storehouse, that there may be meat in mine house, and prove me now herewith, saith the Lord of hosts, if I will not open you the windows of heaven, and pour you out a blessing, that there shall not be room enough to receive it (Mal.3:10)".

Tithing is a test of management and responsibility in handling the things of God. It is a test of honesty, obedience, accountability, love, discipline, diligence, faithfulness, etcetera.

How faithful are you in the management of the time God has given you? A faithful manager of time adds value to his time by using it to create values for others. A faithful citizen of the Kingdom of God maximizes his existence by saving lives and making lives better for other people.

> **The fact of life remains that whatever you have, you are given by God.**
> **The way you manage it determines the type of manager that you are.**

### Are you ready for the next opportunity?

*For the creation waits in eager expectation for the children of God to be revealed. Romans 8:19*

Being a Christian offers a glorious dimension to your lives - "Christ in you, the hope of glory."
Every manufacturer offers something great inside his product.
We all have great talent hidden in our clay jars!
We have the greater one in us waiting to be exposed.
Make up your mind to stop wasting your potentials and opportunities.
Start developing and deploying your talents as from today.
You can combine your employment with preparation to deploy your potential. Do not just work for your boss; mind your own business when you return home. To get more from life, you need to become more.
You need to invest more in yourself than you invest in your job.
You need to start doing that right away. Waiting is wasting.
God gives a new day and new opportunities all the time. Be ready!

## PRINCIPLES: WHAT IS POTENTIAL?

1) Potential is the Maker's deposits in His creatures the necessary abilities and qualities to become self and achieve life purpose.

2) Potential is God's guarantee of a colourful and glorious existence for every man.

3) Potential is God's idea of granting His creatures' relevance and fulfilment.

4) Potential is a hidden capacity to do more than you have already done (Philip.4:13).

5) Potential is God's hidden power in His creatures to resolve earthly challenges (1 John 4:4).

6) Potential is a pointer to your purpose and assignment on earth (Je. 1:5).

7) Potential is the power a thing is endowed with to fulfil its purpose.

8) Potential is a pool of unlimited divine resources residing in you (Eph. 3:20).

9) Potential is a stamp of purpose placed on you as God's package at birth.

10) Mediocrity is living below your potential.

11) The key to fulfilling your life purpose is in discovering, developing and deploying your potential.

12) The greatest tragedy of life is not in dying young but in living long without discovering or fulfilling your potential.

## CHAPTER 2: THE PRINCIPLES OF POTENTIAL

*For the kingdom of heaven is as a man travelling into a far country, who called his own servants, and delivered unto them his goods. 15 And unto one he gave five talents, to another two, and to another one; to every man according to his several ability; and straightway took his journey.* **Matt. 25:14-15**

In addition to showing us the different types of stewardship, Jesus Christ in the parables of the talents also taught us the principles of potential.

## Lessons on potential from the parable of the talents

### 1. The source of all potential is God (Matt. 25:14; Gen. 1:1.)
God is the Source of potential, so we call Him the omnipotent.
It was He that created heaven and earth and everything in them.
Everything before existence and creation existed in God alone.
God, the omnipotent, is the source of all potential and powers.
He is the beginning and the end. He created time and boundaries for mortal men. He is omnipotent for He can do all things and create everything and anything from nothing. There is no limit to God's potential (ability.) He can give life and take life. He can create the universe and destroy it. He can create new things and do what is considered impossible for mankind (Mark 10:27). He can make Sarah, an 89-year-old woman give birth to a mighty man and can make a virgin deliver a baby.
He is God with all potential, and He needs no man's permission to do and undo as He wishes.

### 2. Every man is a steward of God's potential (Matt. 25:14)
We are all managers of God's given potentials.
The talents that are given to the servants belong to the Master, and so are the profits they made with it. Both the stewards and what they own are all owned by the Master (Psalm 24:1).
Whoever you are and whatever you have all belongs to the Lord.
He who owns you owns all that you own!
The Master owns all the stewards and the talents He gave them to trade.
It is only the quality of their stewardship that the Master sets out to measure (1 Cor.4:2).

### 3. We are not all equally endowed (Matt. 25:15)
Though every man is endowed, by God, with potential, we are not all equally endowed. Our potentials are not equal. They are different in types, measures and focus. Even when the potentials are the same, they may come in different proportions for use in different areas of life.

It is to every one according to his or her life purpose. The purpose of every person determines the potentials such receive. God averse waste. He will not give you more resources than you need for your purpose. While it is true that we are not equally endowed with the same resources, it is also true that our purposes and responsibilities are not the same.

### 4. We are all sufficiently endowed for individual purpose.
Even though we are not equally endowed, we are all sufficiently equipped to fulfil our unique purposes.

The Master gave each steward according to his ability. He is not expecting any steward to perform beyond that ability. It took the man with five talents the same time as it took the one with two talents to deliver profits and all expected of the one with one talent is perhaps to raise another one talent. To whom much is given, much is expected and to whom less is given, less is expected.

The master is not demanding from any one of them what He has not endowed them with (Luke 12:48). You see God is not unfair to any.

### 5. Hidden in every potential is unlimited opportunities (Heb. 11:3)
Though it is hard to know the exact value of that one talent, the Bible scholars indicate it is as much as a million dollars in today's currency. Over 90% of the world population could not lay claim that amount even today. Imagine someone burying a million dollar in a bush behind his house?! The servants were all given enough to live productively only that last one was lazy and truly wicked for wasting the opportunity given him. The path of the righteous is created to shine more and more until the final day (Prov.4:18.) An average man has an unlimited supply of vital endowments. Your endowment is a divine entrustment.

The potential of a thing is determined by its source.

You are as dependable as your source. You are as good as your source. In every little is many, and in every small is great (Matt. 25:16).

Genesis 1:28 implies that the ability to have dominion is in every man.

All that we need to do is to be fruitful, multiply, replenish and subdue the earth (womb of the world). Every man has the responsibility to trade the potential deposited within him to enjoy the greatness in his field.
Never despise the day of little beginning (Zech.4.10.)
To be productive, a seed needs to develop and let out the forests inside.
Inside every baby is a man or woman waiting to come out.
Inside a seed of corn is a whole farm of maize waiting to come out.
Every great thing began small. You are worth more than you are and can attain more than you have achieved. There is still more to your life than your present achievements. Ye are gods (Psalm 82:6.) That is mind-blowing. In the beginning, God only existed with everything in existence inside of Him. Never permit what you see to hinder what you are yet to see. God created the things we see from the things we do not see.
So can we. Man is imbued with God's nature and likeness.
Man is inbuilt with God's potential as a God type (Psalm 82:6)
That you cannot see it does not mean that it does not exist.
You are as limitless as your source. Yes, a son of God is a god.

6. **God expects every man to live a profitable life** (Matt. 25:27)
And God blessed them, and God said unto them, be fruitful, and multiply, and replenish the earth, and subdue it: and have dominion. (Gen. 1:28a) God has given every man the mandate to have dominion on earth. He expects us to be fruitful and multiply! God expects profits from all of us having granted us the time and the resources to make a profit for the kingdom of heaven until He returns. It is expected of every man to be a good steward of the resources (talents and time) that God has given by converting unique potential to profitable service.
That step begins with spending time regularly with the Lord.
Sharing an intimate relationship with God makes you more aware of His plan for your life. The best way to find out the full potential of a thing is from the Maker (the Source.) A product's potential and purpose have nothing to do with the opinion of the product, buyers, sellers or other commentators. Until you are very familiar with God's manual for life (Bible), you can hardly maximize your potential. It is like trying to make the best of your smartphone or any other digital devices without reading the manuals. Yes, you can enjoy basic services, but you will never enjoy all the great potential built into the system until you study well the manual.
It is the same with our lives. Unless the word of God refreshes us and directed by it, we will not enjoy the best of our abilities.

Same way every seed needs the right environment to grow into a fruitful tree, God's presence is a fertile environment, required for your potential to grow. God, the source of all potential on earth is your best environment to grow. He is your fertilizer, inspiration, sun, rain and protection-all in one.

> **Man is imbued with God's nature and likeness. Man is inbuilt with God's potential as a God type (Psalm 82:6). That you cannot see it does not mean that it does not exist. You are as limitless as your source. Yes, a son of God is a god.**

### 7. Every talent takes training and time to grow (Matt.13:32)

Your future wealth and greatness are buried inside your talent.
You have to train your talent until it becomes a skill and great expertise. It is the Master's key to help you live a fulfilled life.

The first step in talent development is practice. The first step to living a useful life is to be used. Find a place where you can be used so you can become useful. Serve freely. Freely you are given, freely give.

You will once serve to the level that people will be willing to pay you for your service. Some talented people fail in life because they want to be paid for using their talents from the onset. Nobody pays for unproven talent. You need to prove yourself before you can be approved. People want to see before they pay you. As a young man, do not choose a job that pays you the biggest salary. That is being short-sighted. Rather chose a job that helps you to perfect your potential. Serve free in a place your gift can be groomed to expertise.

Find out the place and the people who can bring out the potential in you so that you can deploy yourself. If all you look for is salary and immediate compensation, you will die unfulfilled. But if becoming wealthy and fulfilled is your goal, you need to deploy the gift in you.

**8. To develop potential is the carrier's responsibility (Gen. 25:16)**
That seed has the potential to produce a forest doesn't mean it will automatically do so. It first needs to be planted and enduring growth. That you are born to be great does not mean you will be.
Though every product is created with sufficient potential to fulfil its purpose, only a person who takes complete responsibility for his or her life can develop his or her potential sufficiently to greater perfection. The Parable of the Talents teaches us that we are here to work while we await the return of the master. Salvation is not meant to be the destination of our faith journey. The Bible says, "we are his workmanship, created in Christ Jesus for good works, which God prepared beforehand, that we should walk in them (Eph.2:10)". We are all created to work diligently for the wellbeing of humanity and for the furtherance of the Kingdom of God.
That you are aware of your potential however is no proof that you will fulfil it. It takes conscious actions consistently directed at developing the potential to release it. It requires taking responsibility to perfect your potential to fulfil your purpose effectively. It takes work to be fruitful!

**9. Fear is a major reason people hide their potential (Matt. 25:25)**
Fear not. The major reason people bury their potential is fear.
That includes the fear of God, the fear of Satan and the fear of man.
Whatever you are afraid of masters you.
The only answer to fear is to amass the courage to face your fear.
Refuse to permit fear to make your decisions for you. Many people cannot explore their potential because of either fear of failure or success. Fear of being mocked or hated. Fear of losing loved ones or being destroyed by the enemy. Fear of shame or that of retribution.
Fear of losing your health, money, job or life. Fear of losing your children, lover or spouse. Fear of judgment from God or punishment from man. Fear (false evidence appearing real) can weigh down people and waste their potential. I will rather live with the knowledge of trying and failing than the regrets of not trying at all. The greatest tragedy in life is not death but living a life deprived of a purpose or achievement.
Fear has one goal, and it is to limit your potential.
Fear destroys your hope and faith and love for God and others.
Fear is a trap of potential. The most excellent cure for fear is to have faith in the Lord. Read the promises of God concerning your life and chose to trust him. Choose to act.

Choose to believe and make a move.
Choose to live a courageous life of faith. Don't be afraid to try and fail. Boldness is not lack of fear. Boldness is simply the ability to move on despite fear and obstructions. If you trust God and have faith in Him. If you believe in your dreams and trust your potentials, you can dare to dance in the storm. As a more than a conqueror, success, like failure can no more halt your progress as you unveil your potential and passionately pursue your purpose. You know that everything will work together for your good. You have nothing to lose by confronting your fear.
We are all seeds of God, carrying enough deposits to cause harvests.
We are all responsible for discovering, developing and deploying the potential deposited in us.
Fear is the biggest threat to your success because it warps your thinking and prevents you from taking the right action.
We are not born with courage, but neither are we born with fear. Maybe some of our fears are brought on by our own experiences, by what someone has told us, or by what we've read and heard.
God has not given us the spirit of fear, but of power, of love and a sound mind (2 Tim.1:7.)

*And unto one he gave five talents, to another two, and to another one; to every man according to his several ability.* **Matt 25:15**

You will be judged by what your gifting and calling equip you to do.
That is good news because the resources you will ever need to fulfil your life are already in you.
Fish needs not to struggle to swim, and birds need no training to fly.
Every seed carries a full-blown plant within it. You only need to discover your endowment in life and distinguish yourself with it.
You do not need to compare yourself to anybody or compete with them. You are born to stand out and not fit in. Shine out, do not sell out.
Refuse to be conformed to the artificial class created by the world system. The world has no class for genius; neither can our standardized system cater to their unique needs. Let yourself free to soar like an eagle. You are born to break every limit, classification and restriction.
Set yourself free. Serve the Lord with the gifts you are given. Fear not!

**10. Greatness in life is attached to diligent use of potentials**
Diligent hands will rule, but laziness ends in forced labour (Prov.12:24)!

Students have often asked me in the Bible School if God is fair to give one person five talents, another one two talents and another one only one talent. That sounds like what you hear outside that the world is unfair since the wealth some kids inherited at birth is more than what hundreds of other people can put together throughout their lifetime.
The same people will not comment on the responsibility that such wealth bequeaths on such inheritors. I said it earlier that God averts waste. He will not give you more than you need to fulfil your purpose.
Even more important is the fact that greatness in life depends more on your diligence than your inheritance and gifting.
How often people come into big money by accident or luck and still lose it easily. If you do not master a process of making money, you will always lose it. Nobody ever got wealthy because of what they have but because of what they do with what they have.
It is your diligent use of talent and not talent itself that determines how wealthy and successful you will be. God's talents are gifts to people.
It is what we do with those talents that are gifts to God.
That was the lesson the steward with one talent failed to learn.

## 11. Untapped potential is proof of laziness (Matt. 25:26)
Be confident that you have all it takes to fulfil all your purpose demands. Our focus should not be on how much our gifts are but the use we put them into. Our focus should not be on how many resources we are entrusted with but on how we use our resources to add values to the life of other people. The Master in the parable was angry with the unprofitable steward for his laziness which was equalled to wickedness. Laziness is a wicked wastage of divine potential!
Waste of potential is an act of irresponsibility
Our God-given resources and talents are responsibilities. When God blesses you with life, talents, health or wealth, you have the responsibility to use them well. You are responsible for what you do with the treasures deposited in you. You will give an account for what you do with your potential. That is where the concept of judgment comes from.
Imagine, many people died and were buried with great dreams that were never achieved, visions that were never pursued, destinies that were never realized and purposes that were never fulfilled.
Yes, the worse wastage in life is untapped potential.
Great tragedy happens when a seed withholds its potential within.

Just like the olive tree that Jesus cursed for refusing to be fruitful, the steward who refused to release the potential in his talent was denied further opportunities. He was judged wicked and lazy for wasting an opportunity to live profitably.

The bad news is that wastage of potential is beyond a personal loss. It is a way of denying the entire world a valuable service that the potential God has deposited in you could have provided.

The purpose of our existence is to shine the glory of the Lord into the darkness of the world. You are the light of the world.

A town built on a hill cannot be hidden.

Refuse to be overcome by evil and evil people around you.

Stand and shine!

## 12. We are stewards who will give an account of potential (Gen.25:19)

God is the source of all resources, and everybody will one day give an account of stewardship to Him. Your spouse, children, business even life are not yours. They are all given to you, and you will once give an account. In the two parables of the talents (Matt.25:14-30; Luke 19:12-28), there was a time the master of the stewards in the story returned and demanded that everyone gives an account of his stewardship. That aspect pertains to all of us who have been given God's resources with which we are expected to trade before His return.

Good use of potential attracts increase (Matt. 25:20-23)

A waste of potential attracts divine punishment (Matt. 25:24)

Good servants received the compliments of the Master.

Productive use of potential multiplies your potentials.

The steward who did not invest his talent dishonours God with his wrong motives and mindsets. He thought that God did not deserve the glory over his existence. The judgment of his Master was to remove his potential and cast him away to utter destruction (Matt. 25:28-30.)

When God returns, do not expect compliments for living longer than others or acquiring material wealth than others. He will judge you according to the performance of the assignment He has given you.

May you hear, "well done my good servant" on that day.

But that means you will have to devote your life to doing the work of God, not yours. You will also have to do it well and not with an ulterior motive. You could be doing the work of God for a selfish reward, and you may be doing the same job for the glory of God. It is a matter of perception and motive. God wants us to genuinely love to do His will.

I hope when the Lord returns; He will find you running the race He has appointed for you. May you not be met running your self-appointed race or another man's race.

## 13. God detests waste (Matt. 25: 30)

Improper use of potential depletes it. An unused or misused potential on the other hand denies and hinders a future of prosperity.

The wasting of a seed is the destruction of forests inside.

By failing to release the potential within his one talent, the lazy servant has committed abortion of purpose.

He had denied the manifestation of all the fruits hidden in that talent and by doing so has denied many people that could have enjoyed the harvest from the talent their blessing. That is why God called him wicked.

Every waste, misuse and lazy use of potential by the receiver is wickedness to the Giver and those meant to benefit from it.

The unused or underdeveloped potential is also a waste.

The future of whatever you do not develop is destroyed.

Whatever you do not serve is forfeited.

Talents that are undeveloped decline. Gifts untraded are wasted. The talent unused is lost. The opportunity unused is lost.

Potential unused is lost. An individual needs to commit to the process of personal development to let out his full potential.

The goal of personal development is to help a man reach his full human potential. A hidden and untapped potential is wasted.

Every man is called to grow his talent!

Worst types of people are saboteurs. They are self-destructive.

Saboteurs work to destroy what they are appointed or employed to build. They will hide their talents and refuse to serve, giving all types of excuse. They thought perhaps they are destroying those who allow them to serve. How daft? The greatest gift anyone can give you is the opportunity to serve. When you waste or abuse that opportunity, you sabotage your claim to harvest and rewards.

The man with a talent thought he was clever than his master and that he was punishing a wicked master. What a shock it must have been for him later to find out that he has just destroyed his chances to become great and relevant in life.

## 14. Service is a step to greatness (Matthew 20:26)

God has given every man a gift to serve while alive.

Every man has the responsibility to choose to serve with her or his gift. Every chance to serve is a step to greatness.

Nothing in nature is created to live for itself alone. Rivers don't drink their water nor do trees eat their fruits. We are all here to serve each other. That is our ladder to a life of relevance, importance and greatness. We all have gifts to serve, and so long you are alive, God's plan is for you to grow from one level to a greater level.

If what you did yesterday still looks big to you, then you have not done much today. The past is a nice place to visit but certainly not a good place to stay. Life destination is being the top in your profession. Every gift has great potential to lead to greatness.

If you quit on your gift, you lose. Quitters are losers. Winners are non-quitters. Success is connected with action. Successful people keep moving and taking steps. They make mistakes, but they don't quit.

**15. It is what you serve in life that serves you  (Galatians 6:7)**

People sometimes seek relevance and significance in the wrong places. Your greatest significance comes from offering a unique service. There is nothing like becoming a global point of reference in your profession but that takes a lot of preparation. Leadership is not a position or a title; it is rather influencing others in your area of gifting and profession. It is about serving others with your talent in the best possible way. Only then can you enjoy great fulfilment.

Everyone in life ends up being served by what they serve.

If you serve in a restaurant, you get paid as a steward.

If you serve the music, you are paid as a musician.

It is also where you serve that your salary will come from.

You attract the greatest reward when you serve in excellence what you are sent to the earth to serve. Let your potential guide your pursuits!

**16. God is the Judge and Rewarder of all services (Matt. 25: 28-29)**

The way we manage our inherent potentials (gifts and talents) determines our rewards in life. Effective management increases a man while mismanagement destroys. All the stewards were rightly judged by the Master according to how they utilized their talents. Remember, we will all be judged not according to what we choose to do with our lives but essentially according to the purpose we are created to fulfil.

a) The Master in this story, representing God surely shows great appreciation and compensation to responsible stewards. A continuous guarantee of a product by its Maker is the best insurance for its wellbeing. You also need to have a continuous good relationship with your Maker to fully your life purpose. Only your continuous connection with Him guarantees that you can maximize your potential to fulfil your life purpose. Once you are disconnected from your Source, you are also disconnected to a large extent from His other vital resources for life. Without God, you can do nothing (John 15:5)!

b) The worse reward for a steward is to be disconnected from the presence of his Master- the Source of his existence (Matt 25:30.) In the story of the Prodigal Son, another story of stewardship, Jesus Christ also taught in the Parable of the prodigal son that being separated from the presence of God is dead. The Father, representing God in the story said, "For this son of mine was dead and is alive again; he was lost and is found – Luke 15:24." The ultimate death taught by the Bible is the separation of a man from God, the Source of life. The prodigal son left the service of the Lord for the world system where he soon ended of dinning with swine. The final portion of every prodigal and unprofitable servant is to be cast into outer darkness, where there shall eternally be weeping and gnashing of teeth.

**God honours increase with more increase**
Only a bad master will honour bad stewards. Never reinforce failure! God is the Lord of harvest who rewards every labourer according to individual faithfulness. He that sows sparingly will also reap sparingly, and whoever sows generously will also reap generously (2 Cor. 9:6.) Nobody can deceive the Lord!
The more your ministry serves God's purpose the more He will reward you with an increase. The greatest reward for stewardship is the continuous relationship with your Maker (Matt 25:23; Luke 19:17-18.) The highest appreciation for every steward is not just promotion and increase but the qualification to abide in the presence of the Master. That grants you access to not only the presence of the Master but to His power and every provision available in Him.

> The worse wastage in life is untapped potential.
> Great tragedy happens when a seed withholds its potential within.
> Just like the olive tree that Jesus cursed for refusing to be fruitful,
> the steward who refused to release the potential in his talent was
> denied of further opportunities. He was judged wicked and lazy
> for wasting an opportunity to live profitably.

### Are you ready to meet the Master too?
It is tragic that the servant with one talent lost his rewards and was still condemned into eternal judgement. But before you blame and accuse him, ask yourself if you are deploying well your talent.

We are all like the three stewards in the talent story!

The earth belongs to the Lord (Psalm 24:1), and He has given each one of us talent to fulfil our purposes. Whatever you do with your talent, remember there will be a day of reckoning with the master.

God took the talent away from the man with one talent and gave it to the one with ten. That is to teach us that, "only those who appreciate what God has given them by trading such will be appreciated by Him."

In the parable, the first two servants offered reliable services while the last one provided an unfaithful service. In reward, the master took the talent which was given to the third (unfaithful) servant and gave it to the one who has ten already. This parable taught that faithful service would lead to increased responsibilities in the kingdom of God, while unfaithful service will only earn condemnation.

## THE PRINCIPLES OF POTENTIAL

1) The source of all potential is God

2) We do not have equal potential

3) Hidden in every potential is unlimited opportunities

4) God expects every man to live a profitable life

5) Every talent takes training and time to grow

6) To develop potential is the responsibility of the carrier

7) Fear is a significant reason people hide their potential

8) Untapped potential is proof of laziness

9) We are stewards who will give an account of potential

10) God detests waste

11) Service is a step to greatness

12) It is what you serve in life that serves you

13) God is a Rewarder of purposeful service

14) Leadership in life is about having dominion over the area of your gifting

## CHAPTER 3: THE ENEMIES OF POTENTIAL

*The path of the righteous is like the morning sun, shining ever brighter till the full light of day.* **Prov.4:18**

Imagine a world where we all live at our full capacity.
What a heaven on earth that would be.
The reason we do not have that scenario as reality is because we have the world filled with enemies of potential. Most people hardly touched their potentials till they are dead and buried, no wonder cemeteries have been referred to as the richest place on earth.
Buried there are many dreams unrealised and potentials unfulfilled! Human potential is a great deposit of treasures for the whole world. The development of your potential is expected to lead you on a progressive journey of enlightenment, excellence and success.
It is left for every one of us to focus on the unique area of calling and gifting and develop it. Accepted, we cannot all be good at everything. Not all of us are endowed to start a personal business, for instance. Some are just meant to support the business and visions of other people and if you discover that to be your talent, train your ability to be a good manager or employee. Not all of us can also be traders, businessmen, professors, teachers, cooks or whatsoever. We all have areas in our lives where our conducts are minimum, medium and maximum.
No man is perfect everywhere!
We are all gifted at something. It is left for individuals to discover the area of his or her unique gifts and talents and develop it.

**Maximize You!**
Potential are guides to areas of your gifting, calling and service. Wisdom demands that you put your major focus and efforts on developing your area of unique advantage. That is the main principle behind the economic theory of specialization of labour.
Everyone is expected to develop and specialize in the best area of talents where he can deliver the best market value and use the rewards he receives from such field to buy goods and services from other people who specialize in the area of his weakness. To be able to maximize your potential, you will foremost need to defeat the enemies of potential.

# 1. STEPPING OUT OF THE DARKNESS OF MEDIOCRITY

*The thief cometh not, but for to steal, and to kill, and to destroy: I am come that they might have life, and that they might have it more abundantly.* **John 10:10**

Though the earth and the fullness there of belong to God, people sometimes act as it belongs to the devil. Even though the Lord has given the earth to the sons of men, many believers, out of ignorance, wander around as if they are the trespassers here.
In reality, we're in that cosmos of the kingdom of God, which is the place of domain that the Lord has given us.
God has given every man dominion on earth. However, despite the availability of God's grace for every man to live a successful life, the enemy is also around to hinder people's progress. There are many hindrances that could limit a person's potential development.
Such enemies of potential include:

- Bad company
- Comparison
- Curses
- Discouragement.
- Disobedience
- Distractions and hindrances
- Fear
- Negative tradition, culture and environment
- Opposition
- Past failures and other bad experiences
- Past success and victory
- Procrastination
- Public opinion and peer pressure
- Sin, temptation and tribulations

Enemies of potential are killers of destinies and assasinators of purpose. They disconnect us from God and hinder us from maximizing our potential. Game of comparison, for instance, is a game of foolishness. What has a car gotten to gain in comparing self to a bicycle or a motorcycle? You should be comparing yourself to yourself only!
If a vehicle should be comparing itself to a motorcycle or bicycle, it will live all its life underutilized though it effortlessly speeds faster than its perceived competitors. Only God can judge right if you are performing

well with your potential or not. We are all created differently from each other. We have different potentials, destinies and purposes.

> **Though the earth and the fullness there of belong to God, people sometimes act as it belongs to the devil. Even though the Lord has given the earth to the sons of men, many believers, out of ignorance, wander around as if they are the trespassers here. In reaality, we're in that cosmos of the kingdom of God, which is the place of domain that the Lord has given us!**

### Stop the compare and blame game!
Our problems and challenges are not the same.
Our tests and examination are not the same.
Our destinations are different from each other.
Of what profit is comparison then?
We had a (drama) skit one day in our church where the cook served some of his guests' forks to eat the salad he was going to serve them. Guess what, the guests that were not served forks were wondering what was wrong instead of waiting to see what they were going to be served. For those served with forks, it was proof that they were going to be served a salad. Some of the guests that day had better food than salad. They were not served forks because they only needed a spoon to eat. You see, what you are equipped to serve with mostly points to the nature of your service. Your potential mostly exposes what your purpose is!
We have different potentials because we have different purposes.
If you were served a spoon rather than a fork, perhaps what is coming your way is a palatable plate of soup rather than a plate of salad.
Be patient and be confident. Do not permit the old experience- made up of past success or failure to hinder your progress.

### 1)  Consciously list sources of your frustrations and hindrances
Are you suffering from selfishness and self-centeredness?
Are you troubled by unforgiveness or bitterness?
Are you limited by your environment or culture?

Social norms can easily make great people normal because of the accepted norms of the environment. Break the norms and rules if you want to break through into the realm of pacesetters and road blazers. Refuse to be another shadow in the crowd. Break away from the queues of mediocre causing holds-up on the road of your life. If you could just speed far ahead, you will find out that you are free of, "go-slow" syndromes in average highways. It takes more efforts to drive to the expressway but once you manage to get there, the efforts will worth its while.

### 2) Seek forgiveness for your past sins and mistakes

*And giving joyful thanks to the Father, who has qualified you to share in the inheritance of his holy people in the kingdom of light. 13 For he has rescued us from the dominion of darkness and brought us into the kingdom of the Son he loves. 14 in whom we have redemption, the forgiveness of sins.* **Col 1:12-14 (NIV)**

If the foundation is destroyed, what can the righteous do? Nothing! Your journey to a fruitful life began with salvation when you chose to relinquish your past sin and be reconciled to God.
Satan came to destroy the first man by plotting his expulsion from the Garden of Eden- the presence of the Lord. He did that by introducing sin into the life of Adam and Eve. He is still doing the same today.
Sin is an ultimate destroyer of potential. Not only does it disconnect a man from his source, God, it also bottled up a man's potential.
Access to Jesus Christ is the highest potential available for any man (1 John 4:4). Without Christ, you can do nothing (John 15:5). You can only do all things through Christ that strengthened you (Philip 4:13).
A man without God, like a fish out of water will die (John 15:5)
Every man who wants to make the best out of his potentials need to turn away from sin and yield life to Jesus Christ.
The step out of darkness into light simply begins with salvation.
The transfer from the limitation and destruction of the kingdom of hell into the kingdom of light and unlimited potential begins with giving back your life to the Creator and Maker of all life. Salvation is about taking conscious action to avoid perdition and to embrace life.
Friends, life is temporary, and death is sure.
To enjoy your full potential in this life and the one to come, you better settle that question of eternity today. Man is a spirit, having a soul and living in a body. What we call physical death is a spiritual transition from this physical world into eternity. Where will you spend your eternity?

Will it be with your Creator (which is what we call paradise) or will it be with the devil, the enemy of your soul (which we call hell)?
You better settle that question of eternity today and live in peace.
Here in Europe, people are security conscious. It baffles me that people who do insurance and reinsurance of material things and temporary existence will not care to insure their eternity.
That is a clear case of pounds foolish, penny wise.

> **The development of your potential is expected to lead you on a progressive journey of enlightenment, excellence and success. It is left for everyone to focus on the unique area of calling and gifting and develop it.**

### 3) Transform your mind

*And do not be conformed to this world, but be transformed by the renewing of your mind, that you may prove what is that good and acceptable and perfect will of God.* **Rom.12:2**

To become good, acceptable and live in the perfect will of God for your life, you will need to transform your mind. That means to change the form by renewing it through the meditation of the word of God. Let your thoughts line up with God's instruction and direction for your life. Consider for a moment, your good attitude to be a yellow cap that makes you see good in anything people do. When you put it on, you just love people, and you are very kind and friendly to them. Consider your bad attitude as wearing a red cap that each time you puts it on, you see fire and blood and feel hatred for everyone. Whenever you put on that red cap, you grumble and quarrel and fight your way through everything. Which cap do you think will fetch you favour and grace?
That is the difference positive thoughts and attitudes can make between living life of success and failure. You can never be greater than your mindset. You cannot radiate and speak light when you fill yourself up with the thought of evil and darkness.
Every journey of greatness begins in your mind.
Even now, you are just a thought away from greatness.

You can think your way out of any bad situation (Prov. 23:7.)
Meditate on good things and of good reports (Philippians 4:8.)
Good reasoning comes from God.

### a) Change your mindset

*As a man thinketh so is he.* **Prov.23:7**

The first thing you need to change in your search for a better life is your mind-set. Nobody can be greater than his mind-set.
As a man thinks so is he. Unless you are tired of where you are, you cannot take progressive steps to the next level.
Life changes begin with a change of mind. The best way to transform your life is to transform your mindset. Your mind is so powerful. Medical Science says that 90% of illnesses are directly caused by persisting levels of stress in our human minds. And we know that at least 90% of all problems in life are occurring because of persisting internal stresses (mentally, emotionally, energetically etc.)
Sometimes we are too busy fighting enemies outside our body forgetting that the most potent enemy is the one inside.
The battle of change begins inside before it can be won outside.
No matter what you change outside, until your change inside, the result is temporary. You may change your country or your personality, but until your mind changes, nothing will change in your life.

### b) Use your imagination

After you have conditioned your mind to think according to God's will for your life, you can begin to use your imagination to preview your future. Your mind is not only the seat of your decision but is also a place for imagination. Calmly permit your mind to travel to the future and see yourself in your dreamt positions. Enjoy it and try to get that picture strongly fixed in your mind. Now return to the present and locate the gap between whom you should be then and who you are now.
Take note of the missing gap and draw a self-development plan to prepare yourself for your future. That is how to take a step into your future.

### c) Create expectation through meditation

Consciously meditate and modify unhelpful beliefs, and embrace the ones that make sense to you. Refuse to submit under false prophecy and

bad culture that take away your hope and bright future. Refuse to listen to preachers that make you feel weak, hopeless and powerless.
Invest in materials that boost your courage and motivate you to take progressive steps forward. The quality of your thought determines the quality of your life. That is why learning the Word of God is a great asset and why the enemy will try to rob you of the knowledge of the scripture. Everything you see in the world as a product or a service began first in thought. Yes, your telephone, television, cars etcetera were once By supporting thoughts with faith infused action, such thoughts have become a reality. What do you passionately think about?
Perhaps you are just one thought away from your breakthrough.
Be careful how you think, so your thoughts do not become a self-fulfilling prophecy. For as he thinks in his heart, so is he. There are certain things you should ban from your thought waves if you want to live a blessed existence. The Bible advises us to protect our mindsets from wrong thoughts for such can easily predetermine our experience.

*Above all else, guard your heart, for everything you do flows from it.*
### Prov 4:23 (NIV)

In preparation to step into the light and dwell there, you should endeavour to clean your heart of all the dark spots infested by evil thoughts. Some of the thoughts you want to get rid should include:

a) Indifference
b) Indecision
c) Procrastination and inaction
d) Doubt
e) Worry
f) Fear and bitterness
g) Frustration
h) Timidity
i) Obsession with Materialism and Mammon spirit
j) Laziness

What are other landmines you noticed in your mind?
Make a list and plan to get rid of them. You are crossing over to the realm of light and that demands that you do not carry extra luggage with you from the kingdom of darkness.

## 2. STEPPING INTO THE LIGHT OF EXPLOITS

*And God said, let there be light.* **Gen.1:3**

God of purpose is a God of order.
There is no accident or coincidence in His conducts.
To solve the problem of darkness, he decreed light.
He refused to acknowledge darkness but focussed all his attention on speaking to being the light. Are you speaking what you want to see?

*And such as do wickedly against the covenant shall he corrupt by flatteries: but the people that do know their God shall be strong, and do exploits.* **Dan 11:32**

*See, darkness covers the earth and thick darkness is over the peoples, but the LORD rises upon you and his glory appears over you.* **Isa 60:2**

As a son of God, you are destined to live as a shining sun amidst the darkness. Your connection to God through the grace of Jesus Christ has come to make you shine in these last days.

### a) You need to walk daily in the Word of God

*But his delight is in the law of the LORD, And in His law he meditates day and night. ³ He will be like a tree firmly planted by streams of water, Which yields its fruit in its season And its leaf does not wither; And in whatever he does, he prospers.* **Psalm 1:1-3**

The person who delights in God's law and meditates on it day and night is destined to shine.
To defeat darkness, you need to be filled with the light of God's word. Darkness cannot overcome darkness. It takes light to overcome darkness. It takes the light of God to overcome the darkness of evil. The illuminating light carried by the word of God is the answer to every darkness of ignorance, failure, sickness and other oppression perpetuated by the enemy. It is that light that shines in darkness and darkness cannot comprehend (John 1:1-5.) God's prominent provision to make you shine in these last days is the knowledge of the word of God. Know it. Meditate with it. Pray with it. Prophesy with it.
The word of God is the carrier of God's forever shining light.

There is great power in it. That light shines in darkness and darkness cannot withstand it (John 1:5.) The enemy, on the other hand, is using ignorance of the word of God to flatter and destroy the destiny of people. Though the enemy is destroying the world with flatteries and lies, those who embrace the truth of the word of God shall be free to do exploits.

### b) You need to maximize the power of fasting and prayer

*"Is not this the kind of fasting I have chosen: to loose the chains of injustice and untie the cords of the yoke, to set the oppressed free and break every yoke?* **Isaiah 58: 6**

Some stubborn situations, problems and demonic attacks will not leave you unless you engage in the spiritual weapon of fasting and prayer to break them. That is like a spiritual double barrel gun built to destroy unusual cases of evil and wickedness.
It often takes a combination of fasting and prayer to break the stronghold of the enemy and enjoy breakthroughs of healing, blessing, an abundance of joy and other provisions of grace that come with the glory of God.
Jabez moved from a life of sorrow and limitation to experiencing a life of exceeding greatness when he engaged God in serious prayer.
From that day, his destiny changed from obscurity to greatness.
The blessing took over the curse and the evil prophecy his mother released upon him at birth.

### c) You need to continue to grow in faith

*For in the gospel the righteousness of God is revealed--a righteousness that is by faith from first to last, just as it is written: "The righteous will live by faith."* **Rom.1:17**

God likes to relate with a man by faith not by sight (2 Cor.5:7.)
Without faith, it is impossible to please God (Heb.11:6.)
Saul's life leaped in greatness as he continued to grow in faith.
The righteous is designed to live by his faith (Romans 1:17.)

### c) You need to walk in the spirit

*So I say, walk by the Spirit, and you will not gratify the desires of the flesh.* **Gal.5:16**

Walking in the spirit is about consciously relying on the Holy Spirit to guide you in thought, word, and deed (Romans 6:11-14).

Every believer is expected to daily walk in the spirit to grow up maturely in the Lord. Not only was Apostle Saul baptized in the Holy Spirit through the laying of the hand of Ananias, but he also went further to be baptized. (Acts 9:18) The evidence of your salvation is your joy at walking no more in the flesh but in the spirit. It is to your advantage to discipline the flesh and learn to walk in the spirit.

### d) You need to belong to a local Church fellowship

*Not forsaking the assembling of ourselves together, as the manner of some is; but exhorting one another: and so much the more, as ye see the day approaching.*
**Heb.10:25**

Your faith walk is never meant to be in solitary.

Though the responsibility to grow mature in the faith is personal, the walk is meant to be among companions. In addition to being directly led by God, you need a fellowship with a Church through which God can be directing your life. Nothing helps a man to grow stronger and faster in faith like fellowshipping with like-minded believers.

How can you claim to belong to the head and refuse to be connected to the body? Every new believer needs to belong as a matter of necessity to a local church. There you will be aided to grow in faith in your walk with the Lord. There, you will be told what to do and be encouraged daily on your journey of life. All you need to do to live in your general calling have already been made available to the body of Christ.

Multiple gifts have been deposited in the Church for your blessing (Eph. 4:11-16.) It is your responsibility to avail yourself of such gifts by regularly fellowshipping with your local Church.

### e) You need to change your environment and companionship

*Walk with the wise and become wise; associate with fools and get in trouble. Proverbs 13:20*

Your destiny is greatly affected by your environment.

No matter what is inside the seed, the environment it is planted will determine how far it will grow. Some environments will kill anything positive in you. It is wise to see your companions as part of your environment for when you relate with wise people you easily get wiser, and if you follow fools, your future is doomed.

### f)   You need to commit to kingdom projects

*The fruit of the righteous is a tree of life, and he that wins souls is wise.* ***Prov.11:30***

Pray for a fresh vision of who you are in Christ. Pray for fresh empowerment. Also, commit to living for the Lord.
Make it your habit to fast and pray for souls to be won.
Evangelism is the first calling and employment of every believer.
Until you find your unique calling, you can engage in this general calling. He who saves a soul is wise and would shine in the kingdom of God.
Fast and pray for your Church to prevail above all the attacks of darkness. Pray for your Pastors and leaders to receive greater grace for kingdom exploits. Pray for all the leaders in your society.
Intercede for all believers suffering persecutions and discriminations all over the world. Pray for God's kingdom to come and to be one of the vessels God can use to do His will on earth.
As you add kingdom needs to your prayer points, expect to receive divine vision and empowerment to do greater exploits.

### Get lighted up!

*You are the light of the world. A town built on a hill cannot be hidden.15Neither do people light a lamp and put it under a bowl. Instead they put it on its stand, and it gives light to everyone in the house16 In the same way, let your light shine before others, that they may see your good deeds and glorify your Father in heaven.* ***Matt 5:14"***

Most importantly, strive to know God (intimate relationship) rather than just learning about God (religion). It takes the knowledge of the Lord to be strong and to do exploit in life (Dan.11:32).
The more you fellowship with God, the more you are filled with His light, and the more light you can carry into the world in your earthen jar.
To overcome hatred, you need to be filled with the love of God.
Hatred cannot drive out hatred; same way anger cannot overcome anger. Only the love of God never fails to overcome all evil.
Let the light of God continue to shine through you in all that you do. However small you conceive the light of God in you to be, let it shine.
The more you shine, the brighter your path becomes.

The Lord has raised you as a shining light to the world. Arise and shine!

## THE PRINCIPLES OF THE ENEMIES OF POTENTIAL

1) The kingdom of God is a kingdom of potential.
2) We have different potentials, destinies and purposes.
3) Your greatness and excellence are buried within your potential.
4) Human potential is a great deposit of treasures for the whole world.
5) Potential are guides to areas of your gifting, calling and service.
6) Enemies of potential are killers of destinies and assasinators of purpose.
7) God of purpose is a God of order.
8) To become good, acceptable and live in the perfect will of God for your life, you will need to transform your mind.
9) The battle of change begins inside before it can be won outside.
10) To defeat darkness, you need to be filled with the light of God's word.
11) Your faith walk is never meant to be in solitary.
12) Your destiny is greatly affected by your environment.

## CHAPTER 4: DISCOVERING YOUR POTENTIAL

*And we know that all things work together for good to them that love God, to them who are the called according to his purpose.* **Rom.8:28**

Every person on earth is on a unique assignment. Everyone has a purpose prepared for him and her before such was born. Your potential holds the key to your bright future. Those who will fulfil their purposes are expected to first take the responsibility to discover the potentials they are endowed with to do it. Let us examine specific ways of discovering your potentials.

1. **Find out from your Maker**

*For I know the plans I have for you," declares the LORD, "plans to prosper you and not to harm you, plans to give you hope and a future. 12 Then you will call on me and come and pray to me, and I will listen to you. Jer.29:11-12 (NIV)*

Which better way is available to know your purpose than seeking the face of your Creator? Then you will call on me and pray to me (Jer.29:12)! Naturally, no product can determine its purpose.
Every product takes its purpose from its Manufacturer.
Genuine self- awareness requires an intimate relationship with God. Only God can reveal to you your purpose. The fastest way of discovering your life purpose is to seek it from your Creator. Study the Holy Bible, pray to God and seek His direction in order not to miss your destination. Knowing God is the most important step in self-discovery. That is why satan is plundering destinies by the deceptive theory of the "Big Bang." The purpose behind the big bang theory is to deny people the connection to God so that they can live a meaningless life of nothingness. The devil knows that any branch that is disconnected from the vine is useless. If you do not know where you come from, then it does not matter where you go or end up. Knowing that God creates us in His image and likeness sets us solidly on a path of excellence.
If you do not believe in God or know who you are in Jesus Christ, how can you strive to live in your new creature status?
If you do not know or believe God, how can you live like Him?
Story of excellence takes two to write- God and you. If God is for you nobody or any situation can be against you (Rom.8:31).

**Have an intimate relationship with God**

*Those who know their God are destined to live in excellence and do exploits.* **Dan. 11:32**

*But seek ye first the kingdom of God, and his righteousness; and all these things shall be added unto you.* **Matt.6:33**

It is not enough to discover your purpose from your Maker, it is equally important to maintain a continuous relationship to guarantee your wellbeing. Any potential, no matter how great, that is not committed to God could easily self-destruct.

Before you begin to invest in anyone's potential, be sure of their faithfulness to God and commitment to your organization.

To reveal the treasure hidden in our earthen vessels and reveal the excellency of the power of God in our lives, our life journey should be built around sharing an intimate relationship with Him. That is what the history of all the great men and women in the Bible taught.

There is no way you will make God first in your life that you will not become the first in your career. Only the people that know their God can be strong and be able to do exploit.

a)   You need to know God as the Source of your potentials.
Knowing God as your source gives you confidence about your potential.
A product's potential is as dependable as the power of its source.
Your potential is therefore as limitless as God your Creator.
The Bible teaches that man came out of God's being (Gen.1:26-28).
You are created in the image of God. That shows you are God-type of being. You are a spirit living in a physical body. You share the same essence with God. You are god (Ps 82:6, John 10:24; 2 Pet 1:3-4).
We are also created in His likeness, so we are creative, loving, forgiving (etcetera) just like Him. We share His nature from creation as we were created from onset in His image and likeness.
We are spiritual beings having a natural experience not otherwise.
With that revelation comes an important realisation. You need to remain connected to the source for His resources to keep flowing into you.
You can only o all things through Christ that strengthens you.
Without Him, you can do nothing.
A thing dies once disconnected from its source. Once you uproot a tree from the soil or take a fish away from the water, you kill it.
The same way, a man disconnected from His Maker, is dead!

b) Knowing God includes knowing His instructions and will.
There is no way you will be led by the Word of God that your life will not be successful. Following the way of the King and sharing an intimate relationship with Him can only elevate you. That is why Jesus Christ instructed us to seek first the kingdom of God and right standing with Him (Matt.6:33). It is no excuse to claim not to know your potential, destiny or purpose in life.
You can already start your journey of excellence by seeking the Kingdom of God and having a personal relationship with Him.
King David didn't know what to exchange his life for as an uncelebrated shepherd. His job was to protect the sheep of his parents with his life. He refused to live a life of obscurity and mediocrity.
He served his father with his very best.
When he had the opportunity to fight for the people of the Lord, he demonstrated the same commitment and steadfastness. He risked his life to save God's people. How often we miss a call to greatness because it looked like a dirty and hopeless task. David's relationship with God set him up for a life of fame.

> **The purpose behind the "Big Bang Theory" is to deny people the connection to God so that they can live a meaningless life of nothingness.**

2. **Seek to understand your potential**

*I praise you because I am fearfully and wonderfully made; your works are wonderful, I know that full well. Ps 139:14*

Your true worth and capacity is determined by your Maker and not by you, your friends, family or your partners.
Many people have been named wrongly and assessed poorly than the Lord created you. Your devalued status is a product of wrong positioning. God create only original masterpieces. One problem we have is that of ignorance of identity and purpose. Can you imagine a fish been given the job to climb a tree? It will look like a natural idiot.

But if you cast that same fish into a sea, you will witness the genius in it. Leadership is not meant to be by force but by an influence generated via your excellence in your area of calling. Don't just go to the market place to make money. Be the expert that reigns there and bring God glory
I once read of a story of a man that bought a cheap canvas from a flea market only to find out that the canvas has beneath an old painting. After careful removal of the surface painting, the original picture was found to be a painting from one of the Europeans' best master artist and was valued at several millions of pounds.
No one knew the true value until the concealment was removed!
The Fall of man and the consequent loss of identity has devalued man that only by reminding ourselves of whom we are in the Lord can we begin to retrace our steps to excellence.
The fallen nature of man has given the man a fallen mindset. Everyone desiring to walk in dominion needs a transformation of the mind.
We need dominion over our imagination (mind) before we can take dominion over our environments. The human biggest problem is not physical opposition but mental slavery. You need to start seeing your potential as God sees it. Do not be conformed to this world, but be transformed by the renewing of your mind, that you may prove what is that good and acceptable and perfect will of God (Rom 12:2.)
He that comes from above is above all (John 3:31.)
Recognize your "Greater identity" in the Lord (1 John 4:4.)
You can do all things through Christ that strengthens you (Philip. 4:13.)

3. Understand the demands of your potential

*This book of the law shall not depart out of thy mouth; but thou shalt meditate therein day and night, that thou mayest observe to do according to all that is written therein: for then thou shalt make thy way prosperous, and then thou shalt have good success.* **Joshua 1:8**

Know your design. It points to your purpose
The purpose of a thing determines the potential deposited in it.
God will not demand from you what He does not design in you.
When you understand that you have been given the capacity to have dominion in your area of influence, it becomes easier to search for an area of your gifting and grow in it. Only a person of understanding can perfect his potential. A fool will die before he can fulfil his potential. Knowing your purpose helps you to discover your potential.

A car drives and an aeroplane flies. A fish can swim, and a bird can fly. Understanding the general principles of God concerning living a successful life and obeying His instructions positions a man for success (Joshua 1:8.). The wise understand that obeying God's direction is for his good (Deut. 28:1-14; Ps.1:1-3.) Every law of God that you break may break you. It takes understanding to build and equip every home.

a)   **Know your limit**
We can do a lot more than we think we can do, but there are a variety of limits that cannot be overcome. At fifty years old, I can no more be the best soccer star in my town any more than I can be a top sprinter no matter how I wish. But I can still be who God creates me to be by developing my gifts and talents.
We need to align our lives with the purpose of its Maker.

b)   **Identify your negative traits and start working on them**
What are the personal faults in your life pulling down your progress? What are the relationships hindering your progress? You need to be honest with yourself by letting go, negative people, dishonest people, discouraging people who continue to halt your life progress.

c)   **Identify what you are to do to reach your destination safely**
Map out your goals and pursue them.
Learn to make the most important thing in your life, the most important thing. Prioritize good health.
Body exercise, the Bible says profits a little. Enjoy that little profit. When you maltreat your body, you will open a door for sickness to ravage you. Take care of your body and saturate your heart in love so that you can live long in good health.

4.   **Know your purpose. It confirms your potential**
Knowing your purpose helps you to know what potential is deposited in you and discovering your potential points you to your purpose. Everything has an inherent potential to fulfil its purpose. God is not obligated to provide for what he does not commission you to do (1 Thess. 5:24). God will not judge you for what He didn't send you to achieve.
Once you understand your purpose, you will find the confidence that you have all it takes to fulfil it. Whatever God calls for he provides for! Your potential answers your provision in life. Until you locate and pursue your purpose, you will never know your true worth.

The world is only paying you for the value of what you work per hour. You are sure worth more than that. Your salary does not determine your worth; it is your purpose in life that determines your real worth.
You are worth more than any man said about you.
Let God be true and every man a liar!
What you cost your Maker and not what your employer pays you determines your true worth. Nobody knows your true worth than your Maker. Moses was being paid a shepherd salary while his real purpose was to become a statesman that will lead his people from bondage.
The journey of purposeful existence begins with the discovery of your potentials.

## Discovering Your Potential with DISC

The DISC personality test, based on Marston's DISC theory, has been used in business and personal applications for over 30 years.
Just like creating infinite new colours by mixing primary colours for painting, DISC personality uses these four basic personality traits of human behaviour and every person has a unique blend.
It's the "colour palette of the personality."
The DISC Theory research that Marston conducted in the 1920s continues today to give us great insight into human behaviour and DISC personality types. DISC theory, researched by Dr William Moulton Marston at Harvard University, is a method of identifying predictable actions and personality traits within human behaviour.
Marston narrowed these predictable personality traits into four DISC personality types.[1]

D –     Dominant
I –     Influencer
S –     Steady Relator
C –     Compliance

Score yourself from 1-5 an add up to find your personality/leadership style[2]

*1 = Never*          *2= Rarely*          My Personality/Leadership Style
*3 = Sometimes*      *4 = Often*

---

[1] https://discinsights.com/disc-theory

[2] Key:   1 = Task,       2= People,       3= Extrovert,      4= Introvert

5 = Always

☐ **1 Total** _____

| | | | | | |
|---|---|---|---|---|---|
| I am assertive, demanding, and decisive. | 1 | 2 | 3 | 4 | 5 |
| I enjoy doing multiple tasks at once. | 1 | 2 | 3 | 4 | 5 |
| I thrive in a challenge-based environment. | 1 | 2 | 3 | 4 | 5 |
| I think about tasks more than others or myself. | 1 | 2 | 3 | 4 | 5 |
| I am motivated by accomplishment and authority. | 1 | 2 | 3 | 4 | 5 |

☐ **2 Total** _____

| | | | | | |
|---|---|---|---|---|---|
| I enjoy influencing and inspiring other people. | 1 | 2 | 3 | 4 | 5 |
| I am optimistic about others. | 1 | 2 | 3 | 4 | 5 |
| I tend to be the life of the party. | 1 | 2 | 3 | 4 | 5 |
| I think about motivating people. | 1 | 2 | 3 | 4 | 5 |
| I am motivated by recognition and approval. | 1 | 2 | 3 | 4 | 5 |

☐ **3 Total** _____

| | | | | | |
|---|---|---|---|---|---|
| I thrive in consistent environments. | 1 | 2 | 3 | 4 | 5 |
| I prefer specifics over generalizations. | 1 | 2 | 3 | 4 | 5 |
| I enjoy small groups of people. | 1 | 2 | 3 | 4 | 5 |
| I prefer being a member of a team. | 1 | 2 | 3 | 4 | 5 |
| I am motivated by stability and support. | 1 | 2 | 3 | 4 | 5 |

☐ **4 Total** _____

| | | | | | |
|---|---|---|---|---|---|
| I typically do not take big risks. | 1 | 2 | 3 | 4 | 5 |
| I love tasks, order, and details. | 1 | 2 | 3 | 4 | 5 |
| I am right most of the time. | 1 | 2 | 3 | 4 | 5 |
| I comply with clearly defined rules. | 1 | 2 | 3 | 4 | 5 |
| I am motivated by quality and correctness. | 1 | 2 | 3 | 4 | 5 |

(1) *It is rare that someone has one personality trait only. You may fall into more than one category. Use your P/L style to locate your traits.*

# Quick Reference Guide DISC

| D \| Dominant | I \| Influencing | S \| Steadiness | C \| Compliance |
|---|---|---|---|
| • Fears being taken advantage of by others | • Fears the loss of social standing | • Fears the loss of security | • Fears risk, making mistakes and criticism |
| • Mastering the difference between seeing problems and tackling challenges | • Mastering the difference between true people connection and contacts | • Mastering the difference between pace of work and consistency | • Mastering the difference between procedures and self-constraints |
| • Responds to results-based communication, forward-looking | • Responds to feelings-based communication, creative problem solver | • Responds to request for help, works for the team | • Responds to fact-based communication, grounds the team with reality |

## If this person is...

- **Extroverted** they will exhibit D/I tendencies.

  or

- **Introverted** they will exhibit S/C tendencies.

## Is this person...

- **People Oriented** they will exhibit I/S tendencies.

  or

- **Task Oriented** they will exhibit D/C tendencies.

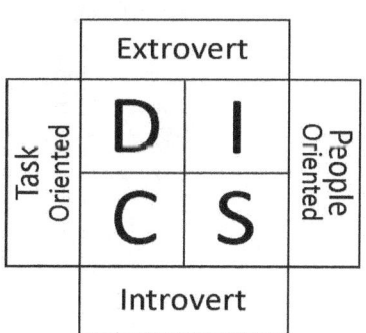

## Notes on DISC

DISC focuses on behaviour not emotions.

DISC is not a clinical tool, so no doctor visits are necessary.

DISC uses four main dimensions and their intensities, so it is a simple language to understand and remember.

DISC does not have a right or wrong, good or bad styles. All styles have strengths and limitations, and all styles are uniquely positive.

DISC can be applied to life. It has practical and useful applications in social, business, and family relationships, and is a good tool for self-development.

## Understanding your personality traits[3]

---

[3] DISC –Church of the Highlands "Growth Track" 2017 edition. Pg 35-41

*"For we are His workmanship, created in Christ Jesus for good works." Eph. 2:10*

Every personality has strengths and challenges.
The following will give you specific areas to focus on to help you work well with others.

"**D**" personalities are dominant, direct, task-oriented, decisive, organized, outgoing, and outspoken. As you embrace these strengths, also make sure to:
- Listen attentively to others.
- Support other team members.
- Invest in personal relationships.
- Balance controlling and domineering tendencies.
- Value the opinions, feelings, and desires of others.

"**I**" personalities are influential, witty, easygoing, outgoing, and people-oriented. As you embrace these strengths, also make sure to:
- Be aware of the tasks that need to be accomplished.
- Balance your emotions, words, and actions.
- Remember to consider details and facts.
- Slow down your pace for others when necessary.
- Listen attentively to others instead of only talking.
- Choose thoughtful decision-making over impulsive decision-making.

"**S**" personalities are steady, stable, analytical, introverted, and people-oriented. As you embrace these strengths, also make sure to:
- Take the initiative.
- Practice flexibility.
- Approach confrontation constructively.
- Be direct in your interactions when necessary.
- Realize change can be healthy, and be willing to adapt.
- Consider the overall goals of your family or group, not just specific processes or procedures.

"**C**" personalities are compliant, competent, task-oriented, goal-oriented, and introverted. As you embrace these strengths, also make sure to:
- Be decisive when necessary.
- Cultivate personal relationships.

- Be open to others' ideas and methods.
- Balance your focus between facts and people.
- Focus on doing the right things, not just doing things right.
- Help others accomplish their goals.

**D**     We are direct and decisive. We are risk-takers and problem solvers. We are more concerned with completing tasks and winning than we are with gaining approval from people. Though the internal drive tends to make us insensitive to those around us, "D"s are not afraid to challenge the status quo, and we thrive when it comes to developing new things. We need the discipline to excel and respond to direct confrontation. Our greatest fear is to be taken advantage of, and even despite our possible weaknesses—which include an aversion to routine, a tendency to overstep authority, an argumentative nature, and a habit of taking on too much—we place a high value on time and use our innovative thinking to accomplish difficult tasks and conquer challenges.

**D/I**     We are curious concluders who place emphasis on the bottom line and work hard to reach our goals. We are more determined than we are inspirational, yet our high expectations and standards for ourselves and those around us typically cause us to make quite an impact, motivating others to follow us. We have an array of interests and can become distracted by taking on too many projects. We often need to focus, prioritize, and simply slow down. Because we thrive on activity and forward motion, we like to accomplish tasks through a large number of people. Joshua (Joshua 1), Noah (Genesis 6-9), Sarah (Genesis 16, 1 Peter 3:6)

**D/S**     We are achievers with an ability to persevere. We are more active than passive, but possess a kind of calm sensitivity and steadiness that makes us good leaders. We seem to be people-oriented but can easily be dominant and decisive when it comes to tasks and project planning. We strive to accomplish goals with fierce determination that comes from a strong internal drive, but we could benefit from contemplative and conservative thinking as well as spending more time focusing on relationships.
Daniel (Daniel 1-6), Job (Job 1:5, James 5:11), Martha (Luke 10:38-42)

**D/C** We are challengers that can either be determined students or defiant critics. Being in charge is important to us, yet we care little about what others think as long as we get the job done. We have a great deal of foresight and examine every avenue to find the best solution. We prefer to work alone. Though we fear failure and the lack of influence, we are motivated by challenges and can often be excellent administrators. We can benefit from learning to relax and paying more attention to people.
Malachi (Malachi 4), Nathan (2 Sam. 12:1-13), Nahum (Nah 1-3)

**I** We are inspiring and impressive. Enthusiastic, optimistic, impulsive, and emotional—we tend to be creative problem solvers and excellent encouragers. We often have a large number of friends, but we can become more concerned with approval and popularity than with getting results. Our greatest fear is rejection, but we thrive when it comes to motivating others. Our positive sense of humour helps us negotiate conflicts. Though we can be inattentive to details and poor listeners, we can be great peacemakers and effective teammates when we control our feelings and minimize our urge to entertain and be the centre of attention. We value lots of human touch and connection.

**I/D** We are persuaders who are outgoing and energetic. We enjoy large groups and use our power of influence to attain respect and convince people to follow our lead. Sometimes we can be viewed as fidgety and nervous, but it comes from our need to be a part of challenges that have variety, freedom, and mobility. We could benefit from learning to look before we leap and spending more time being studious and still. We make inspiring leaders and know how to get results from and through people.
John the Baptist (Luke 3), Peter (Matthew 16 and 26, Acts 3), Rebekah (Genesis 24)

**I/S** We are influential counsellors who love people, and it's no surprise that people love us. We live to please and serve and tend to be good listeners. Looking good and encouraging others is important to us, as is following through and being obedient. We often lack in the area of organization and can be more concerned with the people involved than we are with the task at hand. However, we can be centre stage or behind the scenes with equal effectiveness, and we shine when it comes to influencing and helping others. Barnabas (Acts 4, 9, 11-15), Elisha (1 Kings 19, 2 Kings 2-3), Nicodemus (John 3, 7, 19)

**I/C** We are inspiring yet cautious assessors who are excellent communicators through the combination of concerned awareness and appreciation of people. We excel in determining ways to improve production. We tend to be impatient and critical, and can also be overly persuasive and too consumed by the desire to win. We like to work out of the box, and we could benefit from trying new things and caring less about what others think. This personality type often possesses a gift for teaching; we are generally dependable when it comes to paying attention to details and getting the job done. Miriam (Exodus 15-21), Ezra (Ezra 7-8), Shunammite Woman (2 Kings 4:8-37)

**S** We are steady and more reserved. We do not like change, and thrive in secure, non-threatening environments. We are often friendly and understanding as well as good listeners and loyal workers who are happy doing the same job consistently. With an incredible ability to forgive, reliable and dependable "S"s tend to make the best friends. Our greatest fear, however, is loss of security, and our possible weaknesses naturally include not only resistance to change, but also difficulty adjusting to it. We can also be too sensitive to criticism and unable to establish priorities. To avoid being taken advantage of, we need to be stronger and learn how to say "no." We also like to avoid the limelight, but when allowed to genuinely help others, we will gladly rise to the occasion. We feel most valued when we have truly helped someone.

**S/D** We are quiet leaders who can be counted on to get the job done. We perform better in small groups and do not enjoy speaking in front of crowds. Though we can be soft- and hard-hearted at the same time, we enjoy close relationships with people, being careful not to dominate them. Challenges motivate us, especially ones that allow them to take a systematic approach. We tend to be determined, persevering through time and struggles. We benefit

from encouragement and positive relationships.
Martha (Luke 10:38-42), Job (Job 1:5, James 5:11)

**S/I**  We are inspirational counsellors who exhibit warmth and sensitivity. Tolerant and forgiving, we have many friends because they accept and represent others well. Our social nature and desire to be likeable and flexible makes us inclined to be overly tolerant and nonconfrontational. We will benefit from being more task-oriented and paying more attention to detail. Kind and considerate, we include others and inspire people to follow us. Words of affirmation go a long way with us, and with the right motivation, we can be excellent team players. Mary Magdalene (Luke 7:36-47), Barnabas (Acts 4, 9, 11-15), Elisha (1 Kings 19, 2 Kings 2-13)

**S/C**  We are diplomatic and steady, as well as detail-oriented. Stable and contemplative, we like to weigh the evidence and discover the facts to come to a logical conclusion. More deliberate, we prefer to take our time, especially when the decision involves others. Possible weaknesses include being highly sensitive and unable to handle criticism, and we also need to be aware of the way we treat others. Operating best in precise and cause-worthy projects, we can be a peacemaker; this makes us a loyal team member and friend. Moses (Exodus 3, 4, 20, 32), John (John 19:26-27), Eliezer (Genesis 24)

**C**  We are compliant and analytical. Careful and logical lines of thinking drive us forward, and accuracy is a top priority. We hold high standards and value systematic approaches to problem-solving. Though we thrive when given opportunities to find solutions, we tend to ignore the feelings of others and can often be critical and downright crabby. Verbalizing feelings is difficult for us, but when we are not bogged down in details and have clear-cut boundaries, we can be big assets to the team by providing calculated "reality checks." Our biggest fear is criticism, and our need for perfection is often a weakness, as is our tendency to give in when in the midst of an argument. However, we are thorough in all activities and can bring a conscientious, even-tempered element to the team that will provide solid grounding.
We value being correct.

**C/I** We are attentive to the details. We tend to impress others by doing things right and stabilizing situations. Not considered aggressive or pushy, we enjoy both large and small crowds. Though we work well with people, we are sometimes too sensitive to what others think about us and our work. We could benefit from being more assertive and self-motivated. Often excellent judges of character, we easily trust those who meet our standards. We are moved by genuine and enthusiastic approval as well as concise and logical explanations. Miriam (Exodus 15-21, Numbers 12:1-15), Ezra (Ezra 7, 8)

**C/S** We are systematic and stable. We tend to do one thing at a time— and do it right. Reserved and cautious, we would rather work behind the scenes to stay on track; however, we seldom take risks or try new things and naturally dislike sudden changes in our environments. Precisionists to the letter, we painstakingly require accuracy and fear criticism, which we equate to failure. Diligent workers, our motivation comes from serving others. Esther (Esther 4), Zechariah (Luke 1), Joseph (Matthew 1:1-23)

**C/D** We are cautious and determined designers who are consistently task-oriented and very aware of problems. Sometimes viewed as insensitive, we do care about individual people but have a difficult time showing it. We often feel we are the only ones who can do the job the way it needs to be done, but because of our administrative skills, we are able to bring plans for change and improvements to fruition. We have a tendency to be serious and could benefit from being more optimistic and enthusiastic. Despite our natural drive to achieve, we should concentrate on developing healthy relationships and simply loving people. Bezalel (Exodus 35:30-36, 8, 37:1-9), Jochebed (Exodus 1:22-2:4), Jethro (Exodus 2:18).

## PRINCIPLES FOR DISCOVERING YOUR POTENTIAL

1) Every man on earth is on a unique assignment.

2) Your potential holds the key to your bright future.

3) Every product takes its purpose from its Maker.

4) Your true worth and capacity is determined by your Maker and not by you, your friends, family or your partners.

5) A product's potential is as dependable as the power of its source.

6) Everyone desiring to walk in dominion needs a transformation of the mind.

7) The purpose of a thing determines the potential deposited in it.

8) Knowing your purpose helps you to discover your potential.

9) Leadership is not meant to be by force but by an influence

10) God will not judge you for what He didn't send you to achieve.

11) Your provision in life is answered by your potential.

12) God is not obligated to provide for what he does not commission

> Self-development is another term for potential development. **Capacity development** is the process of revealing your hidden potential. A question of capacity development answers the need for "filling in the gaps" between your present ability and the desired ability to reach your destination. Capacity development is about securing necessary training, education and skill required to realise your potential.
>
> **Solomon Osoko**

# SECTION 2:

## DEVELOPING YOUR POTENTIAL (CAPACITY DEVELOPMENT)

*Very truly I tell you, unless a kernel of wheat falls to the ground and dies, it remains only a single seed. But if it dies, it produces many seeds. John 12:24 (NIV)*

## CHAPTER 5: THE POWER OF POTENTIAL

*Very truly I tell you, unless a kernel of wheat falls to the ground and dies, it remains only a single seed. But if it dies, it produces many seeds. John 12:24 (NIV)*

A seed is a regenerating part of every plant.
Many ignore the power of seeds because mostly they are the part of the fruit you cannot swallow or chew. They are the most potent of those plants that ensure the continuous existence of their species. The seed carries the power of continuation and multiplication of every plant. It is the transgenerational power that guarantees that the planet will continue to exist beyond the present days and seasons.
The future of the plant is not in its juice or tasty flesh but the seed.
God created a seed for the unique purpose of establishing the continuation of a plant through its reproduction capacity.
A plant that has no seed cannot be fruitful beyond a generation.
That means it cannot multiply itself.

## The Power of a seed

God has given you everything you need to do everything you are purposed to achieve. Like a seed, we all carry potentials meant to make a great difference in our existence. So stop searching outward, start looking inward by placing a demand on your potentials.
Nothing illustrates the power of potentials like the role a seed plays in the making of trees and forests.
There are lots of similarities between a man and a seed.

### 1) A seed carries all it needs for existence

*And God said, "Let the earth sprout vegetation, plants yielding seed, and fruit trees bearing fruit in which is their seed, each according to its kind, on the earth." And it was so. The earth brought forth vegetation, plants yielding seed according to their own kinds, and trees bearing fruit in which is their seed, each according to its kind. And God saw that it was good. And there was evening and there was morning, the third day. Genesis 1:11-13*

A seed carries everything it needs inside to fulfil its purpose.
In God's plan, Life begets life.
Living things always give birth to a new life in a continuous process.
Many underestimate the power of a seed because they cannot see what it carries. Because you can't see something doesn't mean it does not exist.

Believe it or not, inside every seed are trees and seeds to create unending forests of trees and seeds that can replicate the family for eternity. Every seed yields tree that bears unending seeds and trees.
That is the law of seed, and that principle applies to every creature of God. To you, it means you are limitless.
You already carry everything you need to prosper in life.
You are your own best resources. All you need to prosper is to develop and serve your potential, the best way possible.
No wonder you are peculiar being created in the image and likeness of the limitless God. That fact however also makes you solely responsible for what you make out of your God-given potential!

**2) A seed is at the mercy of a farmer's vision**

*Very truly I tell you, unless a kernel of wheat falls to the ground and dies, it remains only a single seed. But if it dies, it produces many seeds. John 12: 24*

A farmer needs to be able to have a vision of a seed growing to a tree before he can sow it. The reason many will not sow is that they have not enough faith and vision to see the great harvest it might bring.
Every reality is first conceived inside before it is manifested outside.
Every product is first produced inside before it is externally manifested.
Before God created heaven and earth, they were all inside Him.
Before you were born, you were conceived for about nine months in the womb of your mother. Before any material (be it a house, car etcetera) is produced, it is first created inside the manufacturer's mind.
Your ability to believe God and trust yourself helps you to create an image in your mind without which nothing can be created outside.
Our inability to see something with our eyes doesn't make it any less so.
Stop allowing fears and doubts to hinder your vision from coming true.
Go ahead with faith-inspired action and make your dream come true.

**3) A seed is wired for success**

*As long as the earth endures, seedtime and harvest, cold and heat, summer and winter, day and night will never cease. Gen.8:22*

What seed will become is inborn, and it will naturally become it, so long it follows the necessary process. Its future is already wired into its

genetics (DNA.) Once a seed finds itself in the right environment, it evolves and grows into its self. It becomes so inventive and intuitive. Every external agent (rain, sun) and motivation (fertilizers like mentors) bring improvement and perfection that enhance the ability of the seed to grow into a tree than can bear an "already determined" fruits.
The enemy only uses ignorance (Hosea 4:6) to ruin people's harvest.
The major way a man can destroy his harvest is to refuse to sow his seed.
God gives seed to all and leaves us with the decision to sow or not to sow. Once you eat your seed as the bread you have no claim to harvest (2 Cor. 9:10.) But if you choose to plant your seed, you activate your harvest process as you release your seed to grow and multiply.

### 4) A seed starts small

*Do not despise these small beginnings, for the LORD rejoices to see the work begin, to see the plumb line in Zerubbabel's hand.* **Zech. 4:10**

The kingdom of God is like a mustard seed. It always starts small.
A seed has to complete a process of growth to become a tree.
Every adult is born a baby, and every tree is sown as a seed.
There is a big and mighty church in a rented hall.
Every family starts with a person. Then a couple begets seeds that beget seeds that beget seeds, and before you know it, a nation is born.
That is why every abortion constitutes a mass murder.
You can easily destroy nations of people just by aborting one baby.
A million-member company, ministry or church starts with one person.
That is how God works. He created the whole of mankind from just one Adam. Never despise a humble beginning!
If you do, you will miss the mighty hand of God in your life.
God always hides great things in small things called potential.

### 5) A seed regenerates itself

*And God said, Let the earth bring forth grass, the herb yielding seed, and the fruit tree yielding fruit after his kind, whose seed is in itself, upon the earth: and it was so.* **Gen 1:11**

Every seed carries the ability to regenerate itself.
A seed is the source of new life. It has everything it needs to be.

There is no limit to what seed might become.
In a human seed, you have millions of lives (and nations).
Though it looks small and singular, it can fill the whole world.
A seed's greatest duty is to persevere until it can manifest what is inside.
Every man alive carries a great prospect. Just look inside and bring out whatever your environment may demand.
You carry unwritten books and poems in your mind.
You carry great ideas, dreams and visions inside of you.
Your future is inside of you waiting to be released.

### 6) A seed becomes a tree at the end of the process

*Jesus said, "How can I describe the Kingdom of God? What story should I use to illustrate it? 31 It is like a mustard seed planted in the ground. It is the smallest of all seeds, 32 but it becomes the largest of all garden plants; it grows long branches, and birds can make nests in its shade."* **Mk 4:30-32 (NLT)**

The reason many people fail is that they expect to become great at the beginning of their process. That is a wrong expectation.
God's given vision comes to great fruition only at the end (Hab.2:3.)
Don't give up until you get to the top. In your journey from smallness to greatness, learn to persevere and not give up.
Though you go through pains, troubles and trials in your field keep pressing forward until the very end.
Potential is about what is yet to happen and not what has happened.
You have all the potential you need to enjoy a fulfilling existence.

### 7) God of the harvest is the power behind all process and system

*How foolish! What you sow does not come to life unless it dies. 37 When you sow, you do not plant the body that will be, but just a seed, perhaps of wheat or of something else. 38 But God gives it a body as he has determined, and to each kind of seed he gives its own body. 1 Cor.15:36-38*

God is in control of all process and system.
He has created a system to reward every process of life.
Once you release the potential within you, you are transformed into another person experiencing another level of life. It is required that we all die, not physically, but in a self – sacrificing the process of labour and self-investment. God in His infinite wisdom rewards human efforts.

He will reward each seed according to its body.
In essence, God has set up a system that rewards each person according to their labour in potential. You determine how far you will go in the process of development and investment and God's system supplies you with the befitting rewards. Do not be deceived, God cannot be mocked. A man reaps what he sows (Gal 6:7).

> A million-member company, ministry or church starts with one person. That is how God works.
> He created the whole of mankind from just one Adam.
> Never despise a humble beginning!
> If you do, you will miss the mighty hand of God in your life.
> God always hides great things in small things called potential.

## Understanding your Potential

*Blessed is the man that walketh not in the counsel of the ungodly, nor standeth in the way of sinners, nor sitteth in the seat of the scornful. 2 But his delight is in the law of the Lord; and in his law doth he meditate day and night. 3 And he shall be like a tree planted by the rivers of water, that bringeth forth his fruit in his season; his leaf also shall not wither; and whatsoever he doeth shall prosper. Psalm 1:1-3*

Just like a seed, you also carry the same powerful potential to fulfil your destiny. All you need to do is to reach inward into your potentials and keep releasing them one after another in a fertile environment that guarantee productivity.

### 1) Secure genuine value for your existence

*But his delight is in the law of the Lord; and in his law doth he meditate day and night. Psalm 1:2*

A man that secures his life values from the principles of God is destined to be successful. Whatsoever he does shall prosper!
Following God's principles protect you from destructive people and conducts and solidly plant your feet on the path of victory and success. It gives you valuable goals, priorities and missions to live for. When you

have priority in your life, it helps to focus you on achieving your purpose. You cannot richly live until you have great values to live for. Having a great value to live for is what brings discipline and principles to your life.

One of the major weapons of the enemy against purposeful living is a distraction. Only those who maintain focus can experience a breakthrough. The more you focus on the right thing, the more the bad companies and situation will fall away from your life.

## 2) Recognize and celebrate your difference

*I praise you because I am fearfully and wonderfully made; your works are wonderful, I know that full well. Psalm 139.14*

God made us different one from another.
Your life was never meant to be like that of everyone else.
You are created differently, equipped differently and positioned differently to achieve a unique purpose on earth. It is your difference that distinguishes you. Your difference is for your identity.
It is also to make you relevant.
It is what creates special demands for your service.
You are one in over 7.6 billion people inhabiting the earth today!
To add value to others, you first need to recognize and celebrate your uniqueness and allow it to direct you.

## 3) Understand your unique potential

*Before I formed thee in the belly I knew thee; and before thou camest forth out of the womb I sanctified thee, and I ordained thee a prophet unto the nations. Jeremiah 1:5*

We are not all created for the same purpose.
Know what your purpose is all about. Learn what can work perfectly for you and what can limit your performance,
You are a seed of God with unlimited potential.
Potential is not necessarily money or financial wealth.
Potential is all the resources you have that can be used to improve your performance and productivity.
Every seed carries inside it, trees, and fruits and seeds and those carry many more unlimited and unending trees, fruits and seeds.

Your seed will keep multiplying so long you do not stop working at it. The seeds of the righteous shall be mighty in the land. You are created to be the light that lightens up every darkness around you.

**Be fruitful!**
The purpose of life is not just to relax but to be fruitful.
You won't be happy if you are not fruitful.

### 4) Take hold of your dreams and run with your vision

*I will stand upon my watch, and set me upon the tower, and will watch to see what he will say unto me, and what I shall answer when I am reproved. 2 And the Lord answered me, and said, Write the vision, and make it plain upon tables, that he may run that readeth it.* **Habakkuk 2:1-2**

Your vision is the picture of your future!
A question of vision seeks to answer, "Where am I to go?"
Many business schools and motivational speakers have misled people about what true vision is all about. Many people have been taught wrong to think that vision is about dreaming big and earnestly desiring some type of achievement or distinction, as power, honour, fame or wealth.
That is, however, ambition, not vision.
James Collins and Jerry Porras in their 1994 book entitled "Built to Last: Successful Habits of Visionary Companies", used the term 'Big Hairy Audacious Goal' (BHAG) to encourage companies to define visionary goals that are more strategic and emotionally compelling.
Such goals are to capture great goals that such companies hope to accomplish in the future. The Bible teaches us that vision is about receiving the picture of the future from the Scripture (Bible).
It is about receiving direction for your future from the Lord.
That is why the prophet in the above scripture sought the face of the Lord for direction. You will also need to seek the face of the Lord in fasting and prayer for direction for your life. (Jer. 1:4-12)
What a shame that many have replaced godly vision for human ambition.

## The importance of vision

The simple fact that you cannot pursue a future you do not see emphasises the importance of vision. Receiving your vision from the Lord is a good guarantee that you will not miss your destination.
Vision makes a big difference between existing and living.

The best way to break stagnation in a man's life is to show him a future. Reaching your destination begins with a vision. God had to paint a picture of the future to Abram after his cousin left him to inspire him afresh to move on. A man robbed of vision is robbed of motivation and motion towards his future. Vision is a major source of motivation in life. Locate your assignment. Decide what is important to you in life.

The day you find what is worth dying for or living for is the day you begin to live! Remember that every passing second brings you closer to your departure.

> **You are a seed of God with unlimited potential. Potential is not necessarily money or financial wealth. Potential is all the resources you have that can be used to improve your performance and productivity.**

5)  Never stop developing your potential

*Work hard so you can present yourself to God and receive his approval. Be a good worker, one who does not need to be ashamed and who correctly explains the word of truth.* **2 Tim 2:15 (NLT)**

Study your life manual to be approved. **(2 Tim 3:16-17)**
Also, study your potential. Know your abilities, resources and gifts.
Study the area of your gifting and calling.
Learning adds fatness to your vision.
Learners are leaders. Continuous learners make continuous leaders.
Learning is a capacity building and self-development program.

## PRINCIPLES OF THE POWER OF POTENTIAL

1) The future of the plant is not in its juice or tasty flesh but in the seed.

2) God has given you everything you need to do everything you are purposed to achieve.

3) A seed carries everything it needs inside to fulfil its purpose.

4) A seed is at the mercy of a farmer's vision

5) A seed is wired for success

6) A seed starts small

7) A seed regenerates itself

8) Potential is about what is yet to happen and not what has happened.

9) Your life was never meant to be like that of everyone else.

10) We are not all created for same purpose.

11) The purpose of life is not just to relax but to be fruitful.

12) Your vision is the picture of your future!

## CHAPTER 6: RELEASING YOUR POTENTIAL

*And God said, Let us make man in our image, after our likeness: and let them have dominion over the fish of the sea, and over the fowl of the air, and over the cattle, and over all the earth, and over every creeping thing that creepeth upon the earth.*
*27 So God created man in his own image, in the image of God created he him; male and female created he them. 28 And God blessed them, and God said unto them, Be fruitful...Gen 1.26-28a*

In the story of creation, God always spoke to the source of His creations. To create grass, God spoke to the earth to all materials (Genesis 1:11-25). To create Sun and Moon, He spoke to the sky. To create sea creatures, He spoke to the sea.
However, when it was time to create man, God spoke to Himself.
You see, God created man from Himself. Like begets like!
Man is created in His image and His likeness.
Mankind is God-type. God does not create junks.
You are a god (Psalm 82:6, John 10:34.) A son of God is a god.
Every man is an original work of perfection. Each man is unique.
No one is like you among the over 7.5 billion inhabitants of the world
What trivializes human life is the wrong placement.
When you place a round peg in a square hole, all you have is misfit and discomfort. Frustration is a product of misplacement.
A celebration is the recognition of your importance.
There is greatness all over you. Until you discover your potential and deploy it, you may only be tolerated and not celebrated.

*"God gives talent, work transforms talent into genius."*- **Anna Pavlova**

*"You will be the same person in five years as you are today except for the people you meet and the books you read."* — **Charlie Jones**

"Be fruitful!" is a statement of proof that God has deposited sufficient potential in every human being to have dominion.
God will not command you to do what he has not equipped you to do!
It is now the human responsibility to be fruitful.

The mandate to be fruitful means that God expects the man to take responsibility to develop the potential deposited in him to have dominion on earth. What a challenging revelation!
God intends man to operate the same way He operates.
You are expected to take adequate responsibility to develop your potential into perfection.
We all have the corporate responsibility to release our potential to achieve God's mandate for humanity.
You must refuse to live by accident or chance.

## You are wired for success!

*For I know the thoughts that I think toward you, saith the Lord, thoughts of peace, and not of evil, to give you an expected end. Jeremiah 29:11*

*For the vision is yet for an appointed time, but at the end it shall speak, and not lie: though it tarry, wait for it; because it will surely come, it will not tarry. Habakkuk 2:3*

Every seed is wired by the Creator to be itself. That is a success!
God is interested in the success of anyone that will take the responsibility to pursue his or her purpose to the end.
God expects a man to take the responsibility to live on purpose.
Life is not an accident. Choose to live successfully consciously.
Success happens when preparation meets with opportunity.
Failure happens when we fail to make good use of opportunities.
Failure is recorded when opportunity misses preparation.
The worse you can do to yourself is to abuse or misuse opportunity in life. Have you seen people who refuse to give their best in their working places before? Do you know someone who likes to waste time phoning rather than adding values to his company?
That is someone wasting his or her opportunities thinking he or she is cheating others. Such a person is not only wasting a good opportunity to develop potential, but such a person is also wasting the opportunity to serve people who could take them to their next stage. Joseph was promoted from a prisoner to a Prime minister of a foreign country he came in as a slave because he used well the little opportunity he had to relate with prisoners from the king's palace. Wise people put more value

in the opportunity to work with great minds than on jobs that only offer them the opportunity to earn a higher salary. Your time is limited on earth, and when you are not using it to develop yourself and add values to others, you are wasting it. Always maximize the opportunity given to you to develop yourself.
Stop focusing on temporary gain or comfort.
Be conscious of the bigger picture of your future?
Are you focusing on immediate gain or future wealth?
I have experienced different gifted men of God visiting our ministry.
I have also met a few greedy ones' with integrity deficiency.
They tried to grab everything and people they could lay hands on!
Of course, we take notice and never permit such to return.
We are glad to bring back ministers that operated in integrity.
Are you an opportunist who destroys opportunities or are you a valuable contributor who is in constant demand?
Prepare yourself consciously for a life of exploits!

## Activate your potential

Whatever you have and cannot or will not use is simply useless.
A man refusing to use his potential renders it useless and worthless.
The real tragedy is living without potential or purpose.
Living without potential results in a pathetic and tragic life.
It is like forcing a fish to climb a tree. It makes a natural dummy out of it. But as you release it inside the sea, same fish by activating its potential becomes a genius.
To consciously live a successful life, you need to activate your potential. Potential is your maker's deposit in you to guarantee your success.
Potential is not meant to be stored, reserved or preserved but is rather to be released. The challenge with potential is, it is not intended to be dormant. A dormant potential is wasted potential.
To become useful and compensated, potential needs to be activated. Remove, therefore anything that may hinder the release of your potential. To release your potentials, you have to maximize:

- Make self-discovery
- Take personal responsibility
- Follow the rules
- Stay in the right environment

- Redeem the time
- Keep taking steps of faith
- Maximize your trials and frustration

### (1) Make Self- Discovery

*I praise you because I am fearfully and wonderfully made; your works are wonderful, I know that full well. Psalm 139:14*

Purposeful life begins with self-discovery.
It takes self-discovery to activate your God-given potential and make the best use of available opportunities to fulfil your life purpose.
It is, however, your exploration, not an expectation that determines your discovery. There is no accidental discovery in life. Everything ever discovered was consciously explored by someone.
Every man is responsible for self-discovery. The journey of life fulfilment for every man begins with self-discovery.
You cannot achieve or fulfil what you do not discover and pursue.
In the days of our Lord and saviour Jesus Christ, no one can drive a car or fly aeroplane because they have not grown in the knowledge of the technology we live with. This generation has advanced so much in technology, and that affords us an unprecedented opportunity to be the best of ourselves.

### a) We live in the information age

Now you can communicate with anyone anywhere in the world in a second. Microwaves are there to warm your food in a few seconds. You can surf on the Internet and make instant communication across the globe in minutes. As a student, you can attend online seminars and obtain online degrees. The internet and the advent of social media have given people the ability to rise from the ashes and educate themselves. You can listen to full ivy-league lectures or downloadable textbooks easily. You can read the blogs of the world's most successful people. You can enter the minds of those you'd never get to communicate with otherwise. We have more opportunity to learn and apply more things to the job you work or the business you own, than arguably anyone else in history. You don't have to be one thing anymore; if you have the ambition, you can be and do whatever you want.

b) **We enjoy the best transportation and networks**
Unlike in those days when it can take months to cross continents with the ship, you can arrive anywhere in the world within a day or two by an aeroplane. The entire world has been networked into a global village, and we are all becoming world citizen since the world market has become a turf for the best candidate. We are faced with a great possibility and capacity to change the world and leave a lasting legacy.
All we need to do is take the responsibility!

> There is no accidental discovery in life. Everything ever discovered was consciously explored by someone.
> Every man is responsible for self-discovery. The journey of life fulfilment for every man begins with self-discovery.

(2) **Take personal Responsibility for your potential**

*See, I have given you this land. Go in and take possession of the land the LORD swore he would give to your fathers--to Abraham, Isaac and Jacob--and to their descendants after them."* **Deut. 1:8**

*"Set out now & cross the Arnon Gorge. See, I have given into your hand Sihon the Amorite, king of Heshbon, and his country. Begin to take possession of it and engage him in battle.* **Deut. 2:24**

Do you notice the same procedure in the two scriptures above? Whatever the Lord says, He means.
The omnipotent God is faithful to His promise. Nonetheless, it is required that a man takes the responsibility to activate his faith to receive God's promise. That you have a purpose on earth is not a guarantee that you will fulfil it unless you take responsibility. God's plan for everyone is good, but at best it remains a wish.

## The Power of Responsibility

Until a man takes the responsibility to till the ground and sow his seed, there will be no harvest in the field for him. Only the potential you develop now can reward and serve you in the future.
Responsibility is your ability to respond to a demanding situation. Every Christian is created to be a deliverer, leader and community changer- a light and a salt of the world. It is our corporate responsibilities to make the kingdom of this world the kingdom of our heavenly father. Everyone was born with an element of divinity (since we are created in God's image and likeness)
Each one of us was born with unique traits and ability. All we need to do is to take the responsibility to utilize the power deposits (potential) inside of us to solve the problems surrounding us.
Every man is responsible for his potential.
There is a consequence of what you do and do not do with it.

a)   God's promise will only remain a promise until it is claimed.
It takes the ability to take responsibility to convert the promise of God into a reality (Jer.29:11-12). God is sovereign, but you are responsible! Though God is sovereign (He can do all things) yet He has chosen to give the duty to administer earth to mankind (Psalm 115:16).
This concept of responsibility is a biblical doctrine that differentiates religious people from faithful believers of Jesus Christ. While religious people wait for God to come and do what God has asked them to do, the faithful believers, like Joshua take responsibility to go forward in faith and claim their God-given Promised Lands.

b)   Taking responsibility is about making the best use of opportunities
Opportunity is the greatest gift you will ever have to become anything in this life. The best God can give a man is an opportunity. Whatever you ask from God within your time on earth, He will always answer with an opportunity; to meet a man, to attend school, to start an idea, to turn a new leave etcetera. The best any man can give you in life is an opportunity. What you do with that opportunity is your responsibility. It is an opportunity that we convert to health, wealth, profession, fame and other substance of life.

c)   Preparation is the epitome of taking responsibility
In life, if you fail to prepare, you prepare to fail.
The opportunity will surely come once for both the well prepared people and the ill prepared ones. What they make out of it is their responsibility.

As a creature of choice, you will always have a choice in events of life. For every choice you make in life, there is a consequence
Will you use your power of choice to create new horizons for your life?
Though there is abundance in the universe, what you get out of life is a product of your choice.

**Remain hungry**

*You will seek me and find me when you seek me with all your heart. Jeremiah 29:13*

What you make out of opportunities is a product of your hunger.
How hungry are you to get your life vision fulfilled?
A teacher once demonstrated to his student difference between desire, needs and wants. He pushed the head of the student inside a filled bucket and watched the student first resisting gently and then fighting and crawling upon everything to stay alive. He watched the panicked eyes of the student and said, "when you want anything like you want to breathe, you will surely have it." One way to demonstrate your responsibility is to demonstrate a hunger for whatsoever you are seeking. You are in control of your life, stop complaining as if other people own the control to your life. Stop complaining about the situation, people or your circumstances.
Fight for your life so way you will fight for your breath.
In the school of destiny, there is a difference between desire, needs and wants. You only receive what you deserve not what you desire.
If wants are horses, beggars will ride. God said not those who desire Him, but only those who seek him with all their hearts shall find him!
How often we day dream and desire what we do not want to pay the price for. There is a process to achieve everything in the Lord.
God created a system for everything- solar system, body system, blood system etcetera and it takes the diligent following of process and procedures to claim God's ever available promises.
Never get too satisfied and complacent. Stay hungry.

**(3) Follow the rules**

*Similarly, anyone who competes as an athlete does not receive the victor's crown except by competing according to the rules. 2 Tim. 2:5 (NIV)*

Lawlessness takes away freedom (Gen. 2:16-17).
All manufacturers offer a manual to guide the users of their products on the best and safest ways to use their products. It is the same with man. Our wellbeing is predicated on the observation of God's commandment (Eph. 6:13-18). One of the protections God gives to man is His commandments. God's laws ensure the development of our potentials. Commandments are boundaries within which God expects us to function effectively and maximize our potentials.
God created everything to exist within certain laws and regulations.

**(4) Stay in your ideal environment**

*How blessed is the man who does not walk in the counsel of the wicked, Nor stand in the path of sinners, Nor sit in the seat of scoffers! 2But his delight is in the law of the LORD, And in His law he meditates day and night. 3He will be like a tree firmly planted by streams of water, Which yields its fruit in its season. And its leaf does not wither; And in whatever he does, he prospers. Psalm 1:1-3*

Just as nothing is more instrumental to the growth of a seed like its environment, the type of environment you stay will affect your potential. One of the major factors that will affect you greatly in your environment is the company you keep. You will easily break or conform with rules depending on the type of company you keep.

a)  Watch out for wrong companions
Your companions greatly affect your prospect in life.
A friend of fools shall be destroyed (Prov.13:20).
The reason many Christians malfunction is because they live in the world instead of living in Christ. Though we are in the world, we are not part of the world. We are not to live by the worldly standard but by the heavenly standard.

*Blessed is the man that walketh not in the counsel of the ungodly, nor standeth in the way of sinners, nor sitteth in the seat of the scornful. Psalm 1:1*

Abstain by all means from destiny destroyers. You will be so doing be saving yourself from the future of avoidable sorrows, treacheries and disloyalty. Surround yourself with potential enablers

b)  Spend quality time with your family and the inner circle.

Put around you only those that bring out the best of you. Invest in them, and they'll invest in you. Your spouse is your best prayer partner (Matt 18:18-20). Invest in your relationship. Without peace at home, you can hardly have a genuine focus to give your best to your career.
Friendship is probably the greatest support system in the world, so don't deny yourself the time to develop it. Gather around yourself wise counsels if you do not want to be destroyed (Prov.13.20). Surround yourself with people of faith who can help you to grow in the love and counsel of God. You will need such people in good time and bad time.

c) Guard your potential against weeds, pests and hungry animals
You need to get rid of weeds from your garden if you want your potential to wax strong. There are so many weeds around us all that threaten our potentials. One of them is the wrong value systems in our society. You need to protect your heart from the adverse effects of bad customs, traditions and old practices. Some social and religious rules prevent ladies from becoming leaders for they are only permitted to play secondary roles to men. It is left for you to stay only in an environment that brings the best out of you. Do not stay in an environment where all that the people do is to abuse, misuse and take advantage of you. Everything is designed for an ideal environment. A car inside the sea or an aeroplane inside the sea will malfunction.
Sin is another environment that can contaminate your potential.

d) It takes enabling circumstances to maximize your potentials.
Stay in an ideal environment that brings the best out in you.
Every seed also needs a fertile ground to grow. Find a living Church where the word of God is preached in season and out of season.
God puts all his creatures in an ideal environment. Disaster and death results from leaving your ideal environment.
The wrong environment molests potential.
When you place a fish on the land, it will struggle for a while and die. But when you place the same fish in a sea where its potential permits to reign, it suddenly becomes a natural genius. Though every creature is created with the potential to fulfil its purpose, it needs an ideal environment to blossom. Living outside that ideal environment can cause disaster and death.
The prodigal boy ended up eating with swine in the foreign land.
His destiny got restored as soon as he returned to his father's house.

> In the school of destiny, there is a difference between desire, needs and wants.
> You only receive what you deserve not what you desire.
> If wants are horses, beggars will ride.
> God said not those who desire Him, but only those who seek him with all their hearts shall find him! How often we day dream and desire what we do not want to pay the price for.
> There is a process to achieve everything in the Lord.

### (5) Redeem the time

*Redeeming the time, because the days are evil. Ephesians 5:16.*

Time is God's frame for developing your potential and fulfilling your purpose. We always have to redeem the time for days are evil.
We are to invest time in preparing our potentials so that we can make the best of all opportunities that God will permit to come to our ways. Your time is already tickling so every time not well invested is wasted. Though Jesus Christ lived for only thirty-three years on earth, he could boldly say on the cross, "It is finished."
Jesus Christ had no problem to release His soul on the cross having exhausted all his potentials to fulfil His life purpose. We are all racing against time to release our potentials. You also need to make a conscious decision to maximize your time on earth.
Learn to redeem the time. Aspire also to die empty!

*I shall pass this way but once; any good that I can do or any kindness I can show to any human being; let me do it now. Let me not defer nor neglect it, for I shall not pass this way again.* **Etienne de Grellet**

You only get one chance at this life, for a relatively short amount of time. The human challenge is to become all that you can become.
There is a lot that can be achieved and attained by you.
Many of your dreams are waiting to come alive. If you believe you can. Yes, you can and if you believe you cannot, yes you cannot.

As long as you are alive, there is no limit to what you can dream, think, say or do. However, you have got to make the best of your time. Only death can terminate your potential so make hay while the sun shines. There comes a night time when no man can work again.

### (6) Keep taking steps of faith

*You foolish person, do you want evidence that faith without deeds is useless[a]? 21 Was not our father Abraham considered righteous for what he did when he offered his son Isaac on the altar? 22 You see that his faith and his actions were working together, and his faith was made complete by what he did. 23 And the scripture was fulfilled that says, "Abraham believed God, and it was credited to him as righteousness,"[b]and he was called God's friend. 24 You see that a person is considered righteous by what they do and not by faith alone. James 2:20-24*

You will always need the spiritual tool of faith to harness your potential. God's provision to maximize your potential is called faith (Heb. 11:1-2)
It is by faith we are saved. It is by faith we stand. It is by faith we overcome. It is by faith we are healed. It is by faith we are blessed.
The righteous shall live by his faith (Romans 1:17, Galatians 3:11, Hebrews 10:3, Hab. 2:4).
Everything in the Kingdom of God is only possible by faith (Mk. 9:23).
Without faith, it is impossible to please the Lord (Hebrews 11:6).
Whatever you do that is not of faith is in vain (Rom 14:23b).
However little it is, keep taking steps of faith forward.
Some religious people will only fast and pray, calling God to come and do what He has given them the potential to do. What a shame.
Faith in God has come to provoke us to take action based on the promises of God. Don't just pray, watch and pray.
Work and pray. Faith without work is dead (James 2:14-26).
Only those who desire God's promise deserve to have it. Every man has a role to play in bringing to pass God's promise upon his life.

### (7) Maximize trials and frustration

*Consider it pure joy, my brothers and sisters,[a] whenever you face trials of many kinds, 3 because you know that the testing of your faith produces perseverance. 4 Let perseverance finish its work so that you may be mature and complete, not lacking anything. James 1:2-4*

*And we know that all things work together for good to them that love God, to them who are the called according to his purpose. Rom. 8:28*

God often permits challenges into our lives to stir us up.
The problem with potential is that it remains a potential until it is activated. No matter how great the deposits in your life, it remains dormant until you work on it. The uncomfortable and confrontational moments in our lives are mostly that moment when our destiny is shaped. These are the time the universe opens the door to greatness and tests your courage to walk through.
Until you are tired and fed up of your present circumstances, there is no hope of moving forward in life. That is why God of purpose often permits problems to come to our ways to bring out the best in us. Potentials are mostly released when demand is placed upon it.
It is one of the reasons God permits trials and persecution to come to the ways of believers'. Such situations bring the best out of us most of the time. We are not meant to end the journey in failure.
Failure is rather meant to lead to success (Rom 8.28). A righteous man may fall seven times, but he is expected to rise the eighth time.
Stop running away from problems and trials; consider it a joy!
The examination has come to announce the closeness of your promotion.
No test, no testimony. No battle, no victory. Count it all joy!
Hidden inside every problem is a solution. Count it all joy!
Potential has the answer to every problem. Let every problem provoke you to reach inside for new ideas. You are packed with an endless solution for every possible challenge you will face in life. The same way David had to conquer the Giant to step from being a common shepherd to a statesman walking around the palace corridor; many of the greatest people have climbed their mountain of opposition into their highest promotion.
Don't let the magnitude of your problem scare you.
You are born to solve any problem that comes your way.
You have the mind of Christ. That is a Solution Provider's mind!
Many of what we call trials are greatness disguised in work clothes.

*These have come so that the proven genuineness of your faith--of greater worth than gold, which perishes even though refined by fire--may result in praise, glory and honor when Jesus Christ is revealed.* **1 Peter 1:7**

*All things shall work together for your good so long you love God and continue to pursue His purpose for your life.* **Rom 8:28**

The fire you go through has come to process your potential to perfection. Never permit a problem to make you lose focus of God and your life purpose. There has no temptation taken hold of you but such as is common to man. But God is faithful; He will not suffer you to be tempted beyond that which ye can bear, but with the temptation will also make a way to escape, that ye may be able to bear it (1 Cor.10:13.)
The fire you are going through is a purifying fire. God has promised that he will not permit it to burn you (Isaiah 43:2; 48:10.) Embrace it.
Trials and tribulations in most cases develop a character of success in us. Problem and trials are divine doors to new opportunities. Fear not!
Fear has come to negate your power, love and ability to think soundly (2 Timothy 1:7.) Maximize the moment.
Yesterday is history; tomorrow is a mystery. Only the present counts now. It is your gift to determine your future. Seize the moment!

---

**Potentials are mostly released when demand is placed upon it. It is one of the reasons God permits trials and persecution to come to the ways of believers'.**
**Such situations bring the best out of us most of the time.**
**We are not meant to end the journey in failure.**
**Failure is rather meant to lead to success (Rom 8.28).**

---

## Manifest yourself!

*Then Isaac sowed in that land, and received in the same year an hundredfold: and the LORD blessed him. Genesis 26:12*

Isaac managed to reap bounty harvest in a land of drought and lack because he chose to trust God and initiate a process of harvest.
Without faith, it is impossible to please God. It takes faith to experience God as a rewarder of labour and Lord of harvest (Heb.11.6; Eccl.11:4-6.)

It takes active faith to manifest the harvest hidden inside every seed.
Hidden inside every one of us is a forest of untapped potential.
It takes imagination to see through the seed into the forests inside it.
It takes faith to take action to manifest what is buried inside us.
Inside the murderer, Moses was the Pentateuch (the 5 Old Testament books.) Inside the murderer, Apostle Paul was almost half of the New Testament. Inside the poor shepherd boy named David was a king.
Permit no one to discourage you from pursuing your dream.
Begin to apply the seed principle to change your life for the better.
You have all the resources (spiritual, mental, physical, financial etcetera) to create the life you treasure. It is how you invest your potential that will determine what you have and what you lack. Everything can be a seed.
If you desire to harvest love, you can sow more love into people's life.
If you need more joy in your life, sow it into people's life.
Do unto others as you expect them to do unto you.
And do away with bad people that can ruin your harvest.
Depart from relationships that diminish you rather than build you up. Until wrong people leave your side, the wrong thing will continue to happen. Surround yourself with those that can ignite the fire in you and water the seed of greatness in you to fruitfulness.
Then with the word of God rooted in your heart and the right people stationed around you, you can march into your shining future where the entire creature awaits the manifestation of the sons of God (Rom. 8:19.)
Today is is filled with great opportunities. Maximize it!

---

**Depart from relationships that diminish you rather than build you up. Until wrong people leave your side,
the wrong thing will continue to happen.
Surround yourself with those that can ignite the fire in you and water the seed of greatness in you to fruitfulness.**

## PRINCIPLES FOR RELEASING YOUR POTENTIAL

1) God expects a man to take the responsibility to live on purpose.

2) Success happens when preparation meets with opportunity.

3) The true tragedy is living without potential or purpose

4) Potential is your maker's deposit in you to guarantee your success.

5) Potential is not meant to be stored, reserved or preserved but is rather to be released.

6) Purposeful life begins with self-discovery.

7) Opportunity is the greatest gift you will ever have to become anything in this life.

8) There is a process to achieve everything in the Lord.

9) Lawlessness takes away freedom.

10) It takes enabling circumstances to maximize your potentials.

11) Time is God's frame for developing your potential and fulfilling your purpose.

12) Potentials are mostly released when demand is placed upon it.

## CHAPTER 7: DEVELOPING YOUR POTENTIAL

*For I know the plans I have for you," declares the LORD, "plans to prosper you and not to harm you, plans to give you hope and a future. 12Then you will call on me and come and pray to me, and I will listen to you. You will seek me and find me when you seek me with all your heart. You can have it if you really want it.* ***Jer.29:11-13 (NIV)***

Now that you have discovered your potential, the next step is to create an action plan and strategy to develop it.

Self-development is another term for potential development. Capacity development is the process of revealing your hidden potential.

A question of capacity development answers the need for "filling in the gaps" between your present ability and the desired ability to reach your destination. Capacity development is about securing necessary training, education and skill required to realise your potential.

Ignorance is a robber of vision. Experience teaches that you can never go beyond your knowledge and capacity development in life.

In the physical, your earning mostly is attached to your learning.

Capacity development is about stretching yourself to attain the next level. Jesus Christ, our Lord and Savior, invested 30 years in developing Himself for his ministry of three and a half years. Apostle Paul took time out to prepare for his assignment. (Gal. 1:11-18).

To record success and fulfilment, you will also need to invest in your life. To earn more, you need to become more. The more you develop your potential, the more of yourself you are becoming.

Now that you know what is missing in your skill, attitude and experience, purposefully live to acquire them. You are not born by accident and left at the mercy of circumstances; rather you are an extension of God's image and likeness sent on an assignment on earth.

Chose to live on purpose. It is the only route to fulfilment.

Grow. Learn. Expand your mind.

Learn new things and develop yourself.

You are created in the image of God, so you are not destined for a mediocre existence. You are destined for excellent existence.

You are created for exploits. Your knowledge of God is your empowerment school where you are prepared for a life of exploits.

God is omnipotent, and His purpose for your existence will surely come to pass so long you take the responsibility to play your path.

## Draw Your Action Plan

*And the Lord answered me, and said, Write the vision, and make it plain upon tables, that he may run that readeth it. Habakkuk 2:2*

Planning brings alive your vision.
It makes your vision so clear that one can run with it.
Preparation is a conscious step to navigate into the imagined future.
He that fails to prepare prepares to fail. God planned what He wanted!
Planning is about taking the responsibility to expose your potential.
Preparation is about converting your imagination to pursuable goals.
Your action plan should list your goals with a time limit.
Goal setting helps you to see your vison clearly and to set time of accomplishing it. While imagination creates a mental image of something not present to the senses, goal setting brings it to reality.

### a) Dream it (vision)

*All the land that you see I will give to you and your offspring forever. Gen.13:15*

God is committed to giving you what you can see!
You can accomplish any imagination your mind can conceive.
If you can dream it, you can accomplish it!
Dreams are ways of activating your potentials.
Many people have failed thinking they need special resources like money, skill, education or connection to activate their potential.
That is not true. Many rich people started their business and profession without any of that. However all have one thing in common; they are dreamers who can use their imagination to see the reality of their future.
God imagined in His mind the idea He wanted (Isa 48:13.)
You are created to function like He- being created in His image and likeness. That is why you are always pregnant with ideas.
Never permit lack of money, skill, connection, customers, recognition and other secondary things to deny you the power of imagination.
You don't have to be a professional to build a successful life.
Amateur Noah built the Ark, professionals built the Titanic.
You just need to be the best of yourself and that begins with having a good and healthy image of who you are and what you can become.
Imagination gives you the wings to climb high above the fear, failure, limitation, lack, and climb into the heavenly realm to access God's plan

and program. It affords you the privilege to travel years ahead and see your destination. With it comes fresh motivation and passion for pursuing your vision. Imagination also empowers you to reach down deep into your soul where your potentials are waiting and activate them to pursue your new imagination.

b) **Develop it (goal setting)**

Once you locate your purpose and understand the potential deposited in you to fulfil it, draw a plan to develop yourself. The goal of the plan is to expose you to a relevant environment and people that can feed your potential. The fact of life is that you can do more than you are presently doing. You can earn more than you are presently earning because you can become more than you are. Your income will seldom exceed your personal development. Draw your action plan to push you forward. What you become influences directly what you receive for your efforts. To earn more, you will need to become more. In essence, you should be investing more in your self-development than in your employment if becoming wealthy is one of your goals in life. Only a few people make great wealth through employment. Most do it through deployment. People will employ you at the level of your self-development and pay you a corresponding amount.

If you offer your service as a secondary school graduate, you will be paid like one. If you offer service as a competent university graduate, you will be paid as such. If you serve as a medical nurse or doctor, you will be paid as such. Whatever you become influences whatever you get. Compensation mostly is a measurement of your value.

Nobody can pay another man for his time.

What people pay is for the value you offer them within the hour. The value you offer per hour, however, depends on your self-development and the developed stage of your potential.

Do not permit your temporary situation or past failures to define your personality. Develop your uniqueness because there is only one of you.

c) **Deploy it (pursue it)**

Start taking steps to deploy your potentials. Implement your action plan! Wherever you find yourself, begin to use your potential.

There are general steps to take to break out of the realm of darkness in your life to enter the realm of sunshine and progress.

Use every opportunity in life to serve. To refuse to serve your service is self-sabotage that leads to self-destruct. Wise up. Not to be used is to become useless. Service is the twin brother of blessing.
Never be discouraged however hard and ungrateful people can be.
It is not about them. It is about polishing your gift.
It is about you serving the Master. It is about you deploying yourself. Nurture your potentials through your service till it blossoms, and everyone can begin to recognize who you are and what your purpose is among them.
Speak about it. Let your mouth speak out of the abundance of your heart. God spoke what he wanted (Gen. 1:2; John 1:1-5; Prov. 18:21.) Bible teaches that we should be speaking directly to the source of what we desire to have it. God spoke into the sea to create the fishes and to the sky to create birds. Jesus taught us to speak solutions to problems (Mark 11:22-23) fully trusting God by faith that it shall be done.

d) **Maximize it (review progress)**
Human potential has no limit; so long the person is alive.
What you have achieved is no more potential.
Keep taking steps forward. Yesterday success belongs to yesterday.
Take the next step and move to the next level.
There is always more in the Lord.
Once you are too satisfied with your last achievement, you easily lose passion and motivation to move into the next level of your progress.
You alone determine how much you are paid or how far your labours are appreciated depending on the level of your self-development. The more developed your potential is, the higher your worth in the market place. That is why you are paid better with better education, training and experience. We all have the corporate task of maximizing our potential. Every person must become all that he can become.

---

To record success and fulfilment, you will also need to invest in your life.
To earn more, you need to become more.
The more you develop your potential,
the more of yourself you are becoming.

---

# Becoming a total man

*The path of the righteous is like the light of dawn, shining brighter and brighter until midday. Prov.4:18 (HCSB)*

The path of a believer is destined to shine brighter and brighter! There is no graduation in the school of potential development, only promotion. Becoming total man talks of the pursuits of wellness - a multidimensional, holistic, evolving process of achieving your full potential. The goal of an action plan is to help you become the man who can deliver your dreams – a man whose potential is no more dormant but active. Your action plan helps you set up a system and a process of growth that transforms you from who you are to who you should be to fulfil your purpose. Submitting under the process mapped out by your action plan makes you a better version of yourself.
There are several areas of life your action plan should set up to develop.

- Spiritual
- Soul (emotion, Intellectual & thoughts)
- Physical
- Social
- Vocational
- Leadership
- Financial

Etc.

You should spend time investing in your relevant potentials.
Many excellent books have been written on all these topics. Use them! Let's look cursorily at seven of them.

## (1) Develop your spiritual potential (3 John 2)
God wants the man to be spiritually active. That is why He created man in His image and likeness. Spiritual wellness is being connected to something greater than yourself. It is having a set of values, principles, morals and beliefs that provide a sense of purpose and meaning to life, then using those principles to guide your actions.

**Exercise:**
a) Start your date with power hour. End it with a positive affirmation. The happier you start your day, the brighter the rest of the day will be.
b) Take time to meditate (Psalm 1.1-3). Meditation turns knowledge into understanding. Whether in the morning when you wake up, during your lunch break, or before you go to sleep, take five to 10 minutes to meditate each day. Fitting mediation and relaxation into your lifestyle will free your mind and enhance your spiritual wellness.
c) Fasting and prayer is one discipline common to all victorious Christians.
d) Commit to a local church and deepen intimacy with the Lord (Heb.10:25)
e) Pilgrimage. Getting in touch with places you read about in the Bible can make the word of God come alive for you and enrich your encounter with God. Conforming historical reality can enhance your faith.
f) End your day with power hour

## (2) Develop your soul wellness (3 John 2)

Nothing affects a man's status in life as his soul's wellness.
As a man thinks so is he!
Your soul refers to your areas of intellectual reasoning, emotion and decision making. Find out ways to improve your wellbeing in this area and adhere to doing it. Better soul enhances your chances in life. Only a great soul can enjoy a great existence.
While your born-again spirit is already full of Christ, your soul and body are yet to receive or experience the fullness of Christ. Your soul and body still bear the image of Adam, the fallen man.
Developing your soul is more than praying and fasting and studying the Word of God to spiritually strengthen, develop or educate your inward man. It is rather about purifying your soul or renewing your mind to submit to the direction of the inward man. A mature soul submits under the leadership of the spirit man. As your soul develops in the revelation knowledge of Christ, you begin to think and act more like Jesus Christ. Your thoughts, words, imaginations, understanding, actions and character begin to look exactly like the one of the Lord ( Eph. 1:17- 23; Philip 3:10).

**Exercise:**
a) Enjoy nature. Stop just sitting around your work or in front of a television or computer screen. Experience nature and spend time appreciating your environment and breathing in the fresh air.
Try to do things you love. Make time to do every day the things you love that bring you joy. Create time for such no matter how tight your time is. When we do the things we love, such affect not only our moods but our attitude towards other people.
b) Study and meditate the word of God regularly (Psalm 1.1-3).
We change progressively through studying God's Word (Rom 12:2, 2 Cor. 3:18, 2 Tim 2:15) Soul growth can only happen as our carnal mind is increasingly renewed through constant reading, studying, listening to and meditating in the truths of God's Word.
c) Be an agent of love. Do not just do what you love, be an expression of God's love to your world. Do things because God said it. Pursue to live in peace, love and obedience. Live to demonstrate love for God and your neighbours (Matt.22:37-40).
d) Develop human relationship and networks (Prov. 18:24)
The major ingredient that you need to mix with your potential is a human relationship. We often need people to help us develop beyond ourselves. Because of the relationship Elisha had with Elijah, he was able to enter and practice a great prophetic ministry. Elisha was a business farmer turned mighty prophet. He had the double anointing upon Prophet Elijah's life simply by mastering relationship. Think about that fact for a while? The relationship that some of the disciples had with Jesus Christ changed their status from local fishers to fishers of men.

## (3) Develop your physical potential (1 Tim.4:8)
Physical wellness is the ability to achieve and maintain a healthy quality of life and possesses enough energy to be productive in your daily activities both at work and outside of work.
You don't need to be a marathon runner or weightlifting champion to be physically well. It is sufficient to engage in consistent aerobic and muscle-strengthening activities over time as this can easily contribute to having a sense of physical wellness.

**Exercise:**
Improve your physical wellness by choosing to follow these health-enhancing habits:
- Eat a healthy, well-balanced diet and stay properly hydrated
- Achieve and maintain a healthy weight
- Lead an active lifestyle and engage in a regular physical activity
- Practice sun-protective behaviours: use sunscreen, seek shade and wear sunglasses and a wide-brimmed hat
- Get at least seven hours of quality sleep in a tranquil environment
- Follow regular medical, dental and vision check-ups, accept personal responsibility and care for minor illnesses and seek medical attention when necessary
- Manage stress by altering the situation or your reaction to the situation
- Monitor and manage chronic conditions through lifestyle choices and medication (as determined by you and your physician)

## (4) Develop your social potential (Prov.18:24)

Many are intellectually competent but socially disable.
Social Wellness refers to one's ability to interact with people around them. It involves using good communications skills, having meaningful relationships, respecting yourself and others, and creating a support system that includes family members and friends.
Your attitude determines your altitude in life!
Practice the Golden Rule. It's the ethic of reciprocity, which states "One should treat others as one would like others to treat oneself". How do you want others to treat you? Shower others with this behaviour, and you'll attract more of the same.
Practice the Silver Rule. Related to the Golden Rule, it states "Do not do unto others what you would not have them do unto you". It's to make up for the shortcomings of the Golden Rule. How do you *not* want others to treat you? Make sure you don't do this to others.
If you are a person of social strength, you will enjoy living in harmony with your fellow human beings, developing healthy social behaviours and seeking positive interdependent relationships with others.

**Exercise:**
a) Be a role model. The best way to be a better person is to be a role model for others. How can you be an inspirational guide to others? Live by example. In being a role model, remember it's not about making yourself into someone you're not. You don't have to be a formal teacher to serve as one– The very act of sharing knowledge to someone is already teaching in itself. By teaching others, we become better.
b) Be committed to helping others. Try to ask others if there is anything that you can do to make their day better. This action usually leads to self-fulfilment knowing that you have improved the life of another. Make someone's day a better day.
c) Build a better relationship with others. Become a better friend, spouse, family member, office colleague etc. Make the best of your relationship with other people.
d) Explore diversity by interacting with people of other cultures, backgrounds, and beliefs.

## (5) Develop your professional skill (Prov. 22:29)

Do not be limited by the classical expectation that you must only have one purpose to live for in life. The fact remains that we all have multi-potential. While you may choose to focus on one, you are not limited to using only one of your potential. There are many people doing lots of great things at the same time. I have personally worked as a bank director, pastor, teacher and businessman at the same time. It is not wrong to have many potential or practice them at the same time so long you can run them at the same time. Sometimes you need similar attributes and skills to do lots of different things at the same time. The general experience could help you to practice in different fields. Adaptability is required to stay on track in this century.

**Exercise:**
a) Learn something new. Create daily the opportunity to learn something new about yourself, your career, family or community. Educate yourself about one thing you didn't know, and the result is you will become a better person.
b) Work with a mentor. Great people climb on the shoulder of other giants. Permit others to add values to your life. There's always something we can learn from every one, no matter his/her age,

background or area of expertise. Find a role model. Having a role model gives us a concrete image of who we want to become.
c) Spend more time with people who enable you. Hang out with people who you compatible with, like-minded people, people who are positive, successful, strong achievers and positive for your growth.

## (6) Develop your leadership potential (Philip. 3:13-14)

Leadership is about influencing other people through your service.

You can have a big influence at work if you have a reputation for being a leader in your career. Go extra smile to start and complete new training. It is not enough to start that new career, business or profession but you need to pursue it to the very end. Nothing unlocks your potential like the discovery and pursuits of your purpose. The more you pursue your calling, the more your gifts and potential reveal.

Proverbs 22:29 talks of the blessing of diligence, "A man that is diligent, skilled and obsessed in his profession will stand before kings". In essence, he will be great and well accomplished!

Career development often depends on more than acquiring professional skills. You also need additional soft skills, among which is the ability to lead your team. Since leadership is an act of influence rather than force, it requires experience and training.

**Exercise:**
a) Explore your purpose. Ask yourself: Who am I? What is my purpose? What do I value most? These questions will lead you down a road where you will think more in-depth about yourself and allow you to notice things about yourself that will help you achieve fulfilment.
b) Serve your community. Begin to serve a cause or a community today. Give back to life! Serve with discipline. People will judge your capacity to lead by the amount of discipline you display at work. Demonstrate discipline at work by meeting deadlines, keeping appointments, delivering targets and goals within allocated time etcetera.
c) Keep learning. Leaders are learners. Only those who are a step further can lead others. Learning new things keep your skill relevant, sharp and fresh. It prepares you ahead of potential problems and challenges.
d) Be a role model. A good leader sets a good example for others. Leadership is about inspiring others. A leader is a person who can inspire his team members to pursue passionately their mutual goals.
e) Relate well in a way to inspire and influence others positively.

- Make clear the vision and the purpose of your organisation and the roles individuals play in achieving it. Where rules are broken, enforce consequences. Nothing brings progress like an orderly environment where everyone knows the process of events.
- Keep listening. It takes more than talking to lead others. It takes the art of listening. It is only by listening that you learn to act relevantly at all time. By listening to suggestions, ideas, and feedback from other people, you can always offer acceptable goals that carry along all the team members.
- Be inspiring. Encourage others by acknowledging positive things about them rather than just criticizing them. Where there is a cause for correction, always find a thing to praise them for before correcting them. A man who feels respected will easily respond to correction.
- Replace coercion with influence. Allow people to agree with your decision and carry it out as their own commitment. This is easily achieved if you involve them in the decision making from the onset. Everyone cherishes being part of a great thing.

## (7) Develop your financial potential

Everyone wants to be rich but what is most lacking is the determination to develop financial intelligence. To enjoy financial independence and be the best in your profession, you need training on how to grow your wealth. There is a mindset that the rich possess that sets them apart from others. Wealthy people know how to minimize liabilities and maximize profitability. While the poor hold certain self-sabotaging limiting beliefs about money, the rich hold different views that permit them to glide to the pinnacles of financial freedom. One sure way to develop a rich mindset is to read books written by millionaires and prosperous people and learn to adapt their lifestyles. Wealthy people pursue financial plan daily. We could take a few tips for tasters.

**Exercise:**
a) Save some money. Financially intelligent people consistently save and use it for investment purposes while poor people like immediate gratification.
b) Invest in profitable business. Learn the difference between asset and liability. An asset is an investment that puts money back into your

accounts. You gain from it, be it sales, investment portfolios, or any business venture. Liability is simply anything that takes money out of your pocket and never adds any profit into your account. Liabilities either loose value out rightly or depreciate over time. These types of purchases include automobiles, jewellery, and other luxuries. Rich people like to invest while poor people accumulate liabilities. By this, I mean most of what poor people buy gather loss over time while rich people's investment attracts profits and interest over time.
c) Maximize other people's resources. Wealthy people use other people's resources. They borrow money from banks to make more money. They seek professional service to look excellent and standard. They are always ahead of their peers for using professional skills from experts rather than featuring mediocre services.
d) Rich people do not depend on one source of income. They rather have streams of income. Most poor people have only one source of income.

## Are you ready for your future?

The future is not about a time, a dream or a place to come.
Rather, the future is a process to complete.
It is not a destination, but a journey of several developments.
It is not a dream to awake in but rather a several activities you consciously go through to make your dream come true.
If you need your dream to come true, you will need to wake up and work at it. Great future only awaits those who walk towards it in faith.
Plan, pursue and persist. Those are the steps to your future!

> **Career development often depends on more than acquiring professional skills. You also need additional soft skills, among which is the ability to lead your team. Since leadership is an act of influence rather than force, it requires experience and training.**

## PRINCIPLES FOR DEVELOPING YOUR POTENTIAL

1) Capacity development is the process of revealing your hidden potential.

2) Capacity development is about securing necessary training, education and skill required to realise your potential.

3) To earn more, you need to become more.

4) The more you develop your potential, the more of yourself you are becoming.

5) Preparation is a conscious step to navigate into the imagined future.

6) God is committed to giving you what you can see!

7) Nobody can pay another man for his time. What people pay is for the value you offer them within the hour.

8) Human potential has no limit; so long the person is alive.

9) There is no graduation in the school of potential development, only promotion.

10) Nothing affects a man's status in life as his soul's wellness.

11) Leadership is about influencing other people through your service.

12) The future is a process to complete.

## CHAPTER 8: THE PLACE OF LABOUR

*Seest thou a man diligent in his business? He shall stand before kings; he shall not stand before mean men.* **Prov.22:29**

Diligence promotes a worker into a position of excellence. The greatest challenge you will ever have in life is to learn to serve to the world the best of you without falling for the cheap temptation of living a shadowy existence of a copycat.
Only the truly competent workers will serve kings rather than working for ordinary people.
We saw in the earlier chapters that the pursuits of your life purpose demands not only the discovery of your potential but also its development through a carefully mapped out action plan.
It is not enough to dream if you will not take the responsibility to realise it.
Not all people who are frustrated in life are without vision. Some just do not have the passion or motivation to pursue their vision. And having a vision with no passion for pursuing it is a recipe for frustration.
You have dreamt enough, and that is okay.
You have drawn your action plan, and that is fantastic. Now you need to add labour to it if you do not want your dream to turn into nightmares.
Even God worked out his ideas until they become a reality (Gen 2:2-3). Jesus Christ himself declared, ""My Father is always at his work to this very day, and I too am working (John 5:17)."
Work is a blessing that transforms potential into perfect products.
Take action on your goals and dreams. Do not procrastinate.
There are so many reasons for you to work add in life.

a)   Work is God's methodology to release potential
It requires labour to discover, develop and deploy your potential.
Work is God's way of placing demands on your potential.
No amount of business knowledge or Bible wisdom will work for you if you do not work. Genius is one per cent idea and 99 % perspiration.
That is why work was given to man even before the fall of mankind.
It is in work that every glory hidden in a man is exposed to the world.
It is interesting to know that work came before the fall of man.
Work is the art of releasing the dormant divine deposit in a man.
Deployment of potential is the ultimate purpose of work.
Any work not helping to deploy your potential is a diversion of attention and a big distraction to your destiny and purpose.

b) Labour is the laboratory of success
Living a life of distinction is not just about having a great vision or idea but is rather about labouring to offer excellent service. Labour is the laboratory to develop your potential into a beautiful picture of your future. God puts the first man in the Garden to work so that the wealth and treasure deposited in him could be let out. That is why the master in the parable of the talents called the servant with one talent wicked for being lazy with his talent. It is a sinful thing to be lazy in the kingdom of God. Nothing ruins the ministry of Christ like lazy people occupying position without working hard to add value to themselves or the people they are serving. Such usually end up being rumour mongers or critics, hindering busy people. A lazy hand is a devil's workshop. A lazy man will sooner than later become a devil's advocate. Busy people have no time for gossip.

c) Labour also attracts rewards
Jesus taught His disciples to pray for labourers more than any other thing (Matt 9:37-38). The harvest in the Kingdom of God is forever plenteous only labourers are few.
There could be no harvest without a man following the due process of labouring. God cannot be mocked for whatsoever a man sows same he shall reap. Productive labour will always make a big difference between the poor and the rich. (Prov. 29:13; Prov. 22:2, Prov. 10:4). No wonder that the Bible counsels that whatsoever your hand find to do, do it with all your might (Eccl. 9:10).

d) Diligence makes great
God of the harvest is a lover of labourers. God always use workers. Elijah was busy prowling when God led Elijah to recruit him for ministry. The first set of disciples recruited by Jesus Christ was busy fishermen. Saul of Tarsus was already a workaholic before God converted him into full-time apostolic ministry. Labour, no wonder is proof of faith. The book of James says, "Show me your faith without your works, and I will show you my faith by my works. You believe that there is one God. You do well. Even the demons believe - and tremble! But do you want to know, O foolish man, that faith without works is dead? (James 2:18b-20)."

e) Work enhances purpose and brings fulfilment

Nothing brings joy and fulfilment as productive labour.
That is why it is always a happy thing to complete a project.
You feel the joy of creating results.
While you may need to do some jobs to sustain your life, God's idea behind work is to reveal the hidden potential inside of you.
Work is part and parcel of a valuable life. Since destiny and purpose are delivered within a limited time, work is a means of maximising your life and adding value to your existence and that of others. No wonder the Bible insists that we have to make hay while the sun shines.
Nobody has "forever" to fulfil his life assignment. If you do not want your dream to turn to nightmares, you need to wake up and work it out.

> Living a life of distinction is not just about having a great vision or idea but is rather about labouring to offer excellent service. Labour is the laboratory to develop your potential into a beautiful picture of your future.

## Pursue it!

*Thou believest that there is one God; thou doest well: the devils also believe, and tremble. But wilt thou know, O vain man, that faith without works is dead? James 2:19-20*

The proof of desire is pursuit. Put action behind your intention.
We need to work while it is possible and when it matters.
There will be a time when that chance will no more be there.
The purpose of your potential is to help you add value to your life by adding value to other people.

1. **Serve**

*Therefore, my dear friends, as you have always obeyed--not only in my presence, but now much more in my absence--continue to work out your salvation with fear and trembling. Philippians 2:12*

Every dormant potential is activated through work. A passive seed remains a barren seed so long it refuses to expose its inner potential. Serve your gift. Allow yourself to be used if you do not want to become useless. God gave Adam work to unlock the greatness hidden within him. Your greatness is hidden within your potential.
You need to work too to reveal the greatness inside of you.

2. **Serve diligently**

*Lazy hands make for poverty, but diligent hands bring wealth.* **Prov. 10:4**

Diligence leads to eminence
Once you can pay the price of diligence, promotion awaits you.
If you help people to achieve their goals and satisfy their needs, there is a great chance that they will appreciate, compensate and reward you greatly.
If you love what you do and offer your service passionately, you will soon attract to your business streams appreciative clients.
You are the author of your life, and you are solely responsible for the level you reach in life. Can dedication to your career and service promote you beyond your present level in your organisation?
Self-leadership is an essential part of excellent living.
The Bible instructed us to learn from the ants.

*Take a lesson from the ants, you lazybones. Learn from their ways and become wise! 7 Though they have no prince or governor or ruler to make them work, 8 they labor hard all summer, gathering food for the winter. 9 But you, lazybones, how long will you sleep? When will you wake up? 10 A little extra sleep, a little more slumber, a little folding of the hands to rest- 11 then poverty will pounce on you like a bandit; scarcity will attack you like an armed robber. Proverbs 6.6-11 (NLT).*

Ants are hard-working, patient, team-spirited and well organized.
They are unarguably the most industrious creatures.
Your greatness in life depends more on your diligence than on your gifting. I wholly believe that it is your diligent use of talent and not talent itself that determines how wealthy and successful you will be in life. Nobody ever got wealthy because of what they have but because of what they do with what they have. That is why you people who suddenly get rich through winning lotto or gaining a sudden inheritance quickly become

poor because they have not learned the rigorous process of labouring to earn their keep. Once you master the art of diligence, you can repeat your success story even if you lose your wealth by one reason or the other. That could explain why people born poor become rich by their sheer labour and creativity.

All hard work brings a profit, but mere talk leads only to poverty (Proverbs 14:23.) You work does not only earn your salary and bless others, but it also serves as the major source of good self-esteem and personal and fulfilment. Many people miss the opportunity to be wealthy in life because the opportunity disguises itself as work. It takes work to release, develop and maximize your potential.

### 3. Serve with excellence

*"The saying is trustworthy, and I want you to insist on these things, so that those who have believed in God may be careful to devote themselves to good works. These things are excellent and profitable for people." Titus 3:8.*

Serve your potential at its best.
The practice of excellence breaks the barrier of race, colour and language. Excellent service takes limits away and pushes you into the midst of greatness. Excellence is an international citizen.
Everyone associates with it!
Excellent service is profitable for all people- and that includes you!
The more you work at your potential, the better skills become and the higher the compensation you receive from the people you serve.
The main purpose of your potential is to serve God and mankind. This world and its system are imperfect. Mankind can never attain complete perfection until the second coming of the lord, so there is no end to the development of our potential. Development of potential is a continuous exercise for every man that wants to remain relevant and productive in life. God has left the potential for improvement as a continuous source of livelihood for an industrious man. Fulfilment is attained when a man's potential offers satisfaction to the needs of others. The reason many people feel frustrated is that they do not feel their lives are impacting and blessing other people.

A selfish life can be frustrating. Time and over again, it is proven that great joy results from offering service, supports and succours to others. The more excellent your product and service, the more you are appreciated, and the better you feel.

### 4. Serve with endurance

*For the vision is yet for an appointed time, but at the end it shall speak, and not lie: though it tarry, wait for it; because it will surely come, it will not tarry.*
*Habakkuk 2:3*

Another major reason many people get frustrated in life is that they did not serve their purpose to the end. They lack the endurance to wait to reap the fruits of their labours which are mostly made available at the end. The end of the race is far more important than the beginning thereof. Winning is never about how you start but how you end.
Only those who endure to the end shall be saved.
God is God of the end.
God's blessing yields his complete returns only at the end.
To endure means to persevere, persist and patiently wait to the end. Never permit accident, sickness or failure to stop you. There were people in worse cases who have achieved greater things despite their challenges. Problems are oppositions that can be overcome by courage. I have seen deaf, dumb, crippled and physically challenged people occupying all types of great offices. A human mind cannot be limited by his body or situation. You are more than you can ever imagine.

---

**Your greatness in life depends more on your diligence than on your gifting.**
**I wholly believe that it is your diligent use of talent and not talent itself that determines how wealthy and successful you will be in life.**
**Nobody ever got wealthy because of what they have but because of what they do with what they have.**

## PRINCIPLES OF LABOUR

1) Living a life of distinction is not just about having a great vison or idea but is rather about labouring to offer excellent service.

2) It takes labour to discover, develop and deploy your potential.

3) Labour is the laboratory to develop your potential into a beautiful picture of your future.

4) God of the harvest is a lover of labourers. God always use workers.

5) Nothing brings joy and fulfilment as productive labour.

6) The proof of desire is pursuit.

7) Every dormant potential is activated through work.

8) Diligence leads to eminence.

9) Self leadership is an essential part of excellent living.

10) Your greatness in life depends more on your diligence than on your gifting.

11) The practice of excellence breaks the barrier of race, colour and language.

12) Winning is never about how you start but how you end.

**Self-manifestation** is about revealing your dormant and hidden self through continuous development of your potentials.

It is the pursuits of self-realisation through your daily activities of self-development, improvement and service to others.

It is about manifesting your destiny by aligning yourself to your potential in the journey of becoming your better self.

**Solomon Osoko**

*NIV*

# SECTION 3:

# DEPLOYING YOUR POTENTIAL (SELF MANIFESTATION)

*The path of the righteous is like the morning sun, shining ever brighter till the full light of day. Proverbs 4:18*

## CHAPTER 9: DEPLOYING YOUR POTENTIAL

*The path of the righteous is like the morning sun, shining ever brighter till the full light of day. Proverbs 4:18 NIV*

The plan of God for every man is to shine! To every believer, Jesus Christ said, "You are the light of the world. A town built on a hill cannot be hidden (Matt 5:14)". For every yet to shine believer, the Lord says, "Arise and shine for your light has come, and the glory of the LORD rises upon you (Isaiah 60:1)." Jesus Christ has made the ultimate sacrifice to rescue every believer from the dominion of darkness into the kingdom of light (Col. 1:13).
We are living in an era of glory. All it takes to participate is to sacrifice the old lifestyle to the new one available in Jesus Christ.
The secret of a shining candle, however, is in its sacrifice.
There is first a need to die to the flesh before a person can rise to shine in the Lord Jesus Christ.

*I tell you the truth, unless a kernel of wheat is planted in the soil and dies, it remains alone. But its death will produce many new kernels--a plentiful harvest of new lives. John 12:24 (NLT)*

The multiplication of seed results from self-liberation and not in self-preservation. Unless a seed dies, and let out its potential, it abides alone. The same way you need to die to sinful lifestyle so that you can let out your great potential in the Lord Jesus Christ.
Once you are in Christ Jesus, your potential rises to its highest level.
Greater is he that is in us than he that is the world!
Being in Christ restores you to your destiny of greatness.
Many people in the world just exist; they are not living.
Their potentials are dormant and buried inside them for they have no access to the light that exists only in Jesus Christ.
Many lived as they will never die and died like they never lived.
They lived as if the purpose of life is only to survive.
They are utterly blind to their life's purpose.
Some Christians are not much different.
They still focus on mundane things. They worry over the same stuff that non-believers run after (Matt. 6:25-34). By focusing their life on the minor things of life, they miss the significant things of life.
They miss God and their roles in the agenda of God.

If all you care for is you and your family, you will always live at a lower level of life. No matter how prosperous you think you are at that level, you cannot function at the higher level God wants His sons to function. Your life might prove invaluable not only to God and His kingdom but also to the people you are sent to make a difference in their lives.

For instance, as of today, there are over 821 million hungry people in the world. An estimated sixty per cent of them are women and girls.

And as if that is not painful enough, 3.1 million children under five die due to malnutrition every year.[4]

Now can you feed just a million people out of that number for just one week? Suddenly, all your perceived wealth meltdown to nothing.

Majority of the Christians of the 21st century look like the church in Laodicea that the Lord chastise that, "You say, 'I am rich; I have acquired wealth and do not need a thing.' But you do not realize that you are wretched, pitiful, poor, blind and naked (Rev.3.17)."

How blind have we believers become nowadays? We are so satisfied with eating the crumbs that fall from Pharaoh's table. We have become so lukewarm-neither hot nor cold- like the Church of Laodicea that the Lord promised to spit out. God dislikes mediocre existence.

He demands excellence from us. We carry great potentials and using it only on a cheap lifestyle is bringing God not the glory He truly deserves. So long we continue to live for personal selfish goals; we can hardly rise to the challenge facing the world. So long we only focus on our individual needs; we can hardly deploy our potentials fully.

It takes a world level believer who sees self as a solution provider for his nation or generation to reach beyond selfish personal needs.

It is only at the selfless level that you begin to play a part in God's purpose and agenda for the entire humanity. That is when your potential is deployed at its full level. Nothing leads to the full deployment of our potentials like living for a higher calling and purpose in Christ.

And guess what. All creation is eagerly waiting for the manifestation of the sons of God. It makes you not only a global citizen but a kingdom citizen. Self-manifestation is about revealing your dormant and hidden self through continuous potential development. It is about manifesting your destiny by aligning yourself to your potential in the journey of becoming

---

[4] https://whyhunger.org/just-the-facts/

your better self. It is the pursuits of self-realisation through your daily activities of self-development, Improvement and service to others.

If you see the need for more in your life, you can reach for it!

Your potential can never be fully deployed beyond your perceived need. It is like a man driving to the next street. He has no special energy need. If suddenly he decides to travel to the next city, his motivation and energy level change. If the same man suddenly plans to travel to the neighboring country, his energy level increases all the more.

Now if he decides to travel to a country far away on another continent, his entire body system functions differently. He becomes extra alert and conscious. The body supplies more energy and motivation for a longer journey. Though the man remains the same, the changes in his pursuits have increased the level of his energy supply. The need to perform at a higher level has placed greater demands on his potentials.

The situation is the same with every man in the deployment of potentials. The greater the challenge you face in life, the greater the demand placed upon your potentials.

The greater the responsibility you carry, the more heaven makes way for you so you can accomplish the assignment.

It is a life of waste to life lukewarm and purposeless. The greatest waste in life is not untimely death, but a life lived with aborted potentials.

The burial ground is therefore a well-deserved place for mourning for it is filled with many undeployed or under-deployed potentials.

It is a tragedy to live long with unused potentials and unfulfilled purpose. As an unpublished manuscript, it is an unfinished project for us to live a life of mediocrity despite the existence of the Greater One in us.

Living without deploying your potential is an intentional assassination of your destiny and an unmitigated flunking of purpose.

Every excuse not to deploy yourself is an attempt to veil your existence. It is like walking the street with a mask -covering your real face from the public. Now is the time to run the race of your life with full potential.

> **The multiplication of seed results from self-liberation and not in self-preservation.**
> **Unless a seed dies, and let out its potential, it abides alone. The same way you need to die to sinful lifestyle so that you can let out your great potential in the Lord Jesus Christ.**

## Stepping out

*Many are the plans in a person's heart, but it is the Lord's purpose that prevails Prov. 19:21 (NIV)*

To be outstanding in life, you need to stand out of yourself.
No matter how long you try, you can never deploy your full capacity alone. The truth is God never created you to live alone!
No man is created by God to be an island. You need to work hard to step out of your cocoon and locate yourself in God's purpose
Take away the lid covering your potentials.
Deploying your potential is about running the race of your life with full capacity. Perhaps you have been running at a mediocre level of your potentials because you have been running alone. It is time to increase the tempo by also adding other people's potential to yours.
To deploy your potentials effectively, you need to work with other people. You cannot train to be a professor until other people add to you. You cannot build a tower alone until other people join their efforts to yours. You can hardly reach the peak of any career or project alone without working together with other great minds.
You need other people to train you and to train with you.
You need people to compete with you and to inspire you.
You need people to serve you and to be served by you.
You need to sacrifice your and self-centeredness for the corporate wellbeing of others. You need to go beyond your plans to locate yourself in the purpose of God for humanity.
Until you do that, you will live frustrated and die alone.
No amount of success or wealth can take away that feeling of loneliness and emptiness. God desires you to live a fruitful that impacts the lives of others. Learn the lesson of effective self-deployment from the seed.

### 1) Die to yourself

*He humbled himself in obedience to God and died a criminal's death on a cross. 9 Therefore, God elevated him to the place of highest honor and gave him the name above all other names 10 that at the name of Jesus every knee should bow, in heaven and on earth and under the earth. Philippians 2:8-10 (NLT)*

Unless a kernel of wheat is planted in the soil and dies, it remains alone
The secret of self-deployment is self-sacrifice.

The seed only enters an explosive stage where it yields the harvest of multiple lives when it selflessly sacrifices itself for the wellbeing of others. That was the secret of the greatest man that ever lived.

Jesus Christ died like that proverbial seed, as a selfless service to redeem the entire human race and for that reason; He has been granted the greatest honour available in heaven and on earth.

God will not give you more resources until you have used what you are given. And until you deploy your potential, there is no compensation and recognition. The greatest hindrance to self-deployment is selfishness. Greed and selfishness are some of the worse enemies of progress destroying our generation. Unethical businessmen in the name of making a profit will go to any length to cheat customers.

Employers and employees work against each other instead of working for each other in a win-win atmosphere.

There is no way you can truly deploy your potential until your major motive becomes love for others. Only someone who genuinely loves God and people created in the image of God can selflessly serve others. Profit becomes secondary to such a person.

Only in such loving, selfless, synergic service that greatness is born.

## 2) Work with other people in unity

Miracles happen when people work together as one!

In such an environment, ceilings and limitations are terminated. Miracles begin to happen. Excellent breakthroughs begin to emerge. When men join potential together in unity, greatness happens.

Increase happens. Exploits happen. Every great finding and innovation in human history is a product of synergy. Unity works wonders.

No man is created to live without others. God does not create the man for isolation, and he does not bless a man in isolation.

He told Abraham, "I will bless you so you can be a blessing to others." Nothing hinders a man's speedy progress like isolation.

The key to your next level is with someone. God will use man to bless you same way devil will use men to hinder you. That is where you need to pick your companion well. Satan always uses the same thing God uses to bless to destroy. No one can fulfil his purpose in life in isolation. We are all interdependent. As the body system, though every part is unique and very important, they are all useless without each other. Every part is important but powerless and meaningless without each other.

A hand is useless outside the body, and so is the head.

When all the body parts come together, the body potential suddenly rises to its highest level. We are stronger together.
Like in good melody, we complement each other. The melody from an orchestra can never be compared to a solo instrument.

## The power of synergy

*Truly I tell you, whatever you bind on earth will be[a] bound in heaven, and whatever you loose on earth will be[b] loosed in heaven. 19 "Again, truly I tell you that if two of you on earth agree about anything they ask for, it will be done for them by my Father in heaven. Matthew 18:18-19 (NIV)*

There's hardly anything on earth more powerful than that power of agreement! If any two of you on earth agree as touching anything they shall ask, it shall be done for them by my Father which is in heaven"
Human unity attracts the support and commitment of God.
We see this also in the story of Babel in Genesis 11:6, "Look!" he said. "The people are united, and they all speak the same language.
After this, nothing they set out to do will be impossible for them!"
All the greatest inventions ever created are products of synergies.
A synergy of service is the essence of human potential.
A tree cannot be a forest. A bird cannot make a flock. A fish cannot make a school. A wolf cannot make a pack. A lion cannot make a pride. A single person cannot make a crowd. A man may be able to build his house alone but building a great tower is another thing.
Building great edifices require different talents and skills from diverse professionals. Unity makes human ventures invincible and unstoppable.

## Tips at building synergic force around you

### a) Develop a good relationship with others
There is a great deposit of resources in other people around you.
The key to connecting with other people and unlocking the wealth of potential in their lives is called a relationship. A wealth of resources surrounds every man, but it takes a good relationship to unlock.
We all need to pay good attention to building a good relationship with other people. People tend to do business only with the people they like.

### b) Be a cheerful giver
Stop hoarding things and begin to give at every opportunity to other people. Break the gate of limits upon your life and make yourself God's

distribution agents on earth. Many people have turned themselves to a well that converts every deposit from God to a personal reservoir. God wants us to become a flowing sea through whom He can flow His unlimited wealth into the world. God however is seeking for seas not reservoirs. There is a big blessing in living the life of a cheerful giver. Giving gifts to other people open them up to you.
Give and it shall be given back unto you (Luke 6:38).
The gift of a man open doors for him and grants him access to influential people (Proverbs 18:16).
Every gift of God on people's life can be imparted to you through your relationship with them. Elisha got double anointing upon Elijah's life through his relationship with the anointed man of God.

### c) Live to honour and appreciate other people

Explosive breakthroughs happen within a relationship with other people. Every man or woman is created in the image of God and is created for a purpose. Everyone carries something you need. It is a good and honourable relationship with such people that unlocks the gifts and blessing in their lives to yours. Never underestimate or look down at anybody. People considered Father Abram to be frustrated at the age of 75 years still living under his father's roof with his wife. Now we all sing, "Abraham's blessing is mine". What makes the big difference between Abram and Abraham's life is his relationship with God. Every man carried great destiny. Honour both adults and children. You can learn from everybody and anybody on how to do or how not to do a thing. A child of today will become the grandfather of tomorrow. God does not create junks. Learn to tap into the blessing every creature of God around you carries. Honour people around you if you want to be imparted by the gift they carry. Your family and friends are put around you to encourage, inspire, impart, mentor and support you in your journey of life. They help to relight your candle when your light goes out. There is something in everyone's life for you. It takes honour and appreciation to connect to it. Living an honourable life is the best way to bless your life. Honour begets honour. As you honour them, you will be attracting much honour and blessing into your own life too.

### d) Be involved in mentorship

Mentorship is about gaining from the pain experienced by others. It is cheaper and most gratifying to learn from mentors.

You need to mentor others and permit yourself to be mentored.
Your gifts and potential are for the benefits of other people, the same way the gifts and potential deposited in other people are also for your good. That is why you should always be working in unity with others. God created potentials to work significantly in synergy.

We can save resources perhaps the lives of many youths if we catch them young and mentor them with a wealth of experience life has taught us rather than live them to learn from their own mistakes. I learnt priceless things from my mentors in my early years that helped me to become who I am today.

One mentor told me, "Keep your sight glued to the big picture and at the end line. Have the end in mind than the present. Refuse to choose short-term comforts over long-term benefits." Another one taught me that, "Successful living is a marathon race and not a dash. Therefore, a lifestyle of discipline and principles is required." Another mentor told me, "Do not do short cuts. Nothing puts you on a long line like queuing on a short cut." That advice has saved me great pains many times in the past. Mentorship is a priceless blessing.

### 3) Work with others in alignment with God's will

When we work together in unity, in alignment with the purpose of God, miracles happen. A three-stranded cord is not easily broken.

Potentials transform into epochal breakthroughs when we use our wills to pursue the purpose of God for the world. That is the place church should take the body of Christ and the world as a whole.

That is where the will of God is being done on earth as it is in heaven.

We all have the corporate responsibility to release our potential to achieve God's mandate for mankind.

Unity and synergy are essential for human survival and progress.

Nothing great comes out of the individual selfish effort.

You can join forces with other people of goodwill to fight corruption, crime, terrorism, political, religious and ethnic bigotry; and all type of evil in our society.

## Live full and die empty!

You have come into this world empty and you will depart from it empty. By this I mean you cannot take anything away from it except your good works. Set yourself free from vices of greed, selfishness and materialism. Serve your generation with your full potentials.
Live your life full by giving out all the potentials within you.
Aspire to die empty- having brought out your full potentials.
Love with all your heart. Serve with all your might.
Forgive with all your will. Add value to other people intentionally.
Give your best while you can. Give your best while alive.
Do not give up on your dreams no matter how much you fail. Where there is life, there is hope. Endure whatever you are pursuing to the end. Do not be afraid of making mistakes. Many people have allowed the fear of failure to imprison them and make them live with their lowest abilities. Those are survivals who mistake the goal of life for living safely. The goal of life is more than living safe and secured.
A fulfilled life is more about living fruitful and having dominion
It is about taking all reasonable risks to discover, develop and deploy your potential. Fear has come to limit us from being adventurous, enterprising and daring. It takes courage to bring out the potentials. Courage however does not mean stupidity. Do not be careless.
Many people entrust their vision or resources carelessly in the hands of incompetent and unfaithful people. Some foolishly trust schemers.
Try people before you fully trust them.
Test them before you rest on them. Entrusting your resources in the hands of an untested person is not courage but foolishness.
Courage is about taking a well-calculated risk.
Courage means the determination to face obstacles despite fears.
Set yourself free from the fear of failure. Quite often, failures can serve as incubators for success. So long you learn from your mistake and improve upon it, it is not a loss. Everyone makes mistakes.
Most successful people are those who learn from their mistakes.
The successful people mostly refused to be scared or wrecked by their mistakes but rather learn from it. Successful people are only experts at not making the same silly old mistakes again.

## PRINCIPLES FOR DEPLOYING YOUR POTENTIAL

1) The plan of God for every man is to shine!

2) The secret of a shining candle is in its sacrifice.

3) The multiplication of seed results from self-liberation and not in self-preservation.

4) Your potential can never be fully deployed beyond your perceived need.

5) To be outstanding in life, you need to stand out of yourself.

6) To deploy your potentials effectively, you need to work with other people.

7) God will not give you more resources until you have used what you are given

8) Miracles happen when people work together as one!

9) There's hardly anything on earth more powerful than that power of agreement!

10) The key to connecting with other people and unlocking the wealth of potential in their lives is called relationship

11) Mentorship is about gaining from the pain experienced by others.

12) When we work together in unity, in alignment with the purpose of God, miracles happen.

# CHAPTER 10: PROTECTING YOUR POTENTIAL

*For the gifts and calling of God are without repentance.* **Rom. 11:29**

As the Creator, God is the source and the sole provider of potentials. He is faithful to His gifts.
He does not retrieve His gifts and callings.
Only death can terminate your potential.
Failure cannot terminate your potential. Some of the time, failure can even provoke the improvement and development of your potential.
Age does not terminate one's potential. Abram at his old age started a fresh life of exploits in the Lord. His encounter with God changed his frustration to an intergenerational celebration. He was living with his parents with his wife at the old age of 75 years.
No one talks about his earlier failure and frustration anymore.
Everyone now claims Abraham's blessing.
It took the personal encounter with God - a situation that refreshed his imagination and renewed his focus - to reset his life towards a path of uncommon greatness. God never quit on a man's potential, so long he is alive. Age stage, sickness, failure- nothing can negate potential.
No matter the setback you may witness, so long there is life there is hope. Potential throughout the journey of life remains God's deposit of solution, an ever-available answer to any question of life.
However, as a custodian of potential, it is your responsibility to protect your life (the container of potentials) and all the potentials you carry.

## Protect your potential

Life is a container of potential.
Death is the only terminator of that potential.
God does not revoke potential from a person.
Only the death of a man can terminate his potential.
The termination of potential is the death of purpose.
The end of life is the same thing as the end of potential .
Once potential is destroyed, a purpose is denied of being fulfilled.
That is why the enemy is attacking you with sickness and death.
He knows once he can steal your health and kill your body, he has destroyed your purpose in life and eternity (John 10:10).
The death of a seed is simply the termination of the forest!
That it is why it must remain your daily priority to protect your life and potentials if you want to fulfil your life's purpose.

When an aeroplane or a house is destroyed or damaged by fire, such can no more fulfil its purpose. That is the same way sickness can limit your purpose and death can terminate all possibilities and opportunities.
The day you die is the day your potential is permanently terminated.
Refuse to abort your purpose by protecting your life and your potential.

### a) Abide in your right environment

Every seed is greatly affected by its environment.
That is why a good farmer tills and fertilizes his ground ahead of sowing. The seeds that bear a good harvest in Jesus parable of the Sower were the seeds that fell on the good grounds. The only man that will prosper is the man that locates the self in a good environment where God can bless him (Psalm 1:1-3). It is every man's responsibility to stay in the environment where you feel blessed and loved no matter the trials and tribulations the enemy may bring your way.
The enemy, in a bid to ruin you will first try to uproot you from your right environment. He knows that if he can uproot you from the right environment where God planted you, he can easily sabotage your purpose and ruin your existence. You should know better than him.
Fight for your marriage. Fight for your family. Fight for your church.
In a short period after the Prodigal Son left the comfort zone of his father's house, he started dinning with swine. No matter what he did, nothing prospered- having left his rightful environment.
His frustration only terminated after he returned to his God-given environment. Many people have ruined their destinies for leaving the place of their blessing. They though the grasses outside their environment were greener. The fact remains that not every environment is equally productive to every seed or plant. Some environments bring the very best out of you while some destroy. Locate yourself only in an environment where you are challenged to do exploit. It is mostly the environment where you are celebrated rather than tolerated.
Is there meaningful progress in your life since you have left your old environment for the new one? If yes, abide there.
If not, come back to your senses like the prodigal son and run back home. It takes rootedness in your environment to be fruitful.
Every seed needs a fertile land to germinate and grow.
It takes a good environment to grow to maturity and fruitfulness.
Only a fool leaves a blossoming environment for a bad one.
Abide in the fertile environment where God has placed you!

> Life is a container of potential.
> Death is the only terminator of that potential.
> God does not revoke potential from a person.
> Only the death of a man can terminate his potential.
> The termination of potential is the death of purpose.
> The end of life is the same thing as the end of potential.
> That it is why it must remain your daily priority to protect your life and potentials if you want to fulfil your life's purpose.

b) **Refuse your potential from being contaminated**
Sometimes, if the enemy finds it difficult to uproot you from a fertile place, he will resort to attacking your character so that he can corrupt your personality. He knows that a corrupt tree can only bring forth corrupt fruit. Jesus Christ clearly explained it that, "Make a tree good and its fruit will be good or make a tree bad, and its fruit will be bad, for a tree is recognized by its fruit (Matt.12:33)."
The brother of the Prodigal son though stayed in his environment but he got his attitude messed up. Doubt, anger, envy and other character traits ruin his joy in the middle of abundance. While focussing on the little buckets of blessing that his younger brother took and wasted in a foreign land, he lost sight of the ocean of blessing flowing around him.
His character flaws blinded him to an unlimited sea of potentials surrounding him. The enemy's attack on your attitudes is meant to ruin your potential and affect your altitude.
Sometimes, social media can corrupt your good manners through unsolicited information, posters, misinformation etcetera.
Watch out for those little foxes, before they ruin the vineyard.
Bad company corrupts and evil communication spoils good manners.
Remember that for any wrong action there are consequences.
Beware of being fooled by Satan through evil motivation.
Every blessing from Satan is a trap for your destiny (Prov.37:1-6).
There is no free launch even with Satan.
Such evil blessings will always attract punishment from heaven.
The satanic motive behind such wrong actions and misdeeds is to contaminate and corrupt your potentials. It is also to destroy your integrity from people and discourage them from been attracted to you.
If the enemy can contaminate your potential, he can delay your purpose.

Moses anger, in the Bible, contaminated his leadership potentials and when he lost control once and murdered one of the citizens molesting his brethren, he was forced to flee his country and spent the next forty years of his life as a refugee. His restoration to leadership at the age of eighty took a special intervention of God himself.

### c) Protect your potential from being terminated

The enemy's ultimate goal for contaminating your potential is to terminate your life purpose. He can achieve that by aborting your visions and goals for life or by taking your life- the container of your potentials. It is your responsibility to protect your life and potential from all the attacks of the enemy. Whatever you want to achieve has to be done while you are around and alive. Salvation, for instance, is only available while you are alive (2 Cor.6:2). There is no transfer after death.

Abortion of potential and death of a person achieve the same goal of destroying a person's purpose in life. Your potentials are given to you to fulfil your life purpose so protect them as much as you protect your life. Failure to do that may abort the purpose for your existence.

Even worse, it may have a bad effect on the potentials and purposes of other people connected to you.

Thank God that Joseph didn't die in prison before he became the Prime Minister of Egypt. Imagine what the situation would have been had Herod managed to murder Moses or Jesus Christ? Imagine what could be the fate of the present day believers if Apostle Paul – the author of almost half of the New Testament- had died as Saul without having an encounter with Jesus Christ. We need to fight at all time to secure and protect our potentials.

The war against your potentials is more than a battle for your existence; it is an attack against God's hidden treasures inside of you and a battle against the lives of other people connected to yours in heaven's agenda.

## Uproot the root of destruction

*For the flesh lusteth against the Spirit, and the Spirit against the flesh: and these are contrary the one to the other: so that ye cannot do the things that ye would. 18 But if ye be led of the Spirit, ye are not under the law. 19 Now the works of the flesh are manifest, which are these; Adultery, fornication, uncleanness, lasciviousness, 20 Idolatry, witchcraft, hatred, variance, emulations, wrath, strife, seditions, heresies,*

*21 Envyings, murders, drunkenness, revellings, and such like: of the which I tell you before, as I have also told you in time past, that they which do such things shall not inherit the kingdom of God. Gal 5:17-21*

*Let us not be desirous of vain glory, provoking one another, envying one another. Gal 5:26*

The "flesh" is our natural human nature with its natural tendency to sin. The "flesh" refers to our fallen self-centred nature and is sometimes called "the old man" or "the Adamic nature".

Even our very kind actions can sometimes be tainted by selfishness and become expressions of the flesh.

The flesh has a bent toward rejecting authority; it tends to be lazy and slothful; it is against the things of the spirit and easily resist the purpose of God for your life. A man living in the flesh operates under instincts like with animals' instincts. A person living under the influence of the flesh cannot effectively develop his potentials.

We have to understand that our old human nature is not the way God likes or created it. It is the result of the sin that Adam and Eve permitted into their life, which affected every human being after.

*For they that are after the flesh do mind the things of the flesh; but they that are after the Spirit the things of the Spirit. 6 For to be carnally minded is death; but to be spiritually minded is life and peace. 7 Because the carnal mind is enmity against God: for it is not subject to the law of God, neither indeed can be. 8 So then they that are in the flesh cannot please God. 9 But ye are not in the flesh, but in the Spirit, if so be that the Spirit of God dwell in you. Now if any man have not the Spirit of Christ, he is none of his. Romans 8:5-9 (KJV)*

When we live after the flesh, we do whatever we feel like doing. Without conscience, we may just lie, steal or rob other people of what belongs to them without any conscience. Such behaviour comes from our flesh. Since Adam and Eve fell in the Garden of Eden, the unregenerate man (not born again) lives under the control of his natural senses of sight, feeling, taste, touch and hearing.

The unregenerate human heart is the most deceitful of all things, and desperately wicked (Jeremiah 17.9). Until a man relinquishes the life in the flesh, his potentials are extremely limited. I can use the law of gravity to explain figuratively what happens to such a person.

> **The war against your potentials is more than a battle for your existence; it is an attack against God's hidden treasures inside of you and a battle against the lives of other people connected to yours in heaven's agenda.**

Sin like the law of gravity has come to pull a man living under the flesh down. Nobody can stop the law of gravity.
The only time you can make the law ineffective is when you apply another law, for instance, the law of flying. Since the law of flying is stronger than the law of gravity, an aeroplane can easily lift up itself rather than falling. That is what happens to a man who chose to live under the laws of the spirit of life in Christ Jesus.

*But when you are directed by the Spirit, you are not under obligation to the law of Moses Gal 5:18(NLT).*

*For the law of the Spirit of life in Christ Jesus hath made me free from the law of sin and death. Rom 8:2*

Every believer is a seed of God. He is an eagle born to soar.
All your potential needs to peak is to subject it under a higher law.
When we are born-again, and we allow the law of the spirit to take over, a new law comes to operate in our lives, a heavenly law that lifts us into the graceful arms of Jesus Christ.
This new law of the spirit imbibes us with great potentials to do great and mighty things that we cannot do before. We are now expected to do great exploits since we now possess the mind of Christ.
You, dear children, are from God and have overcome them because the one who is in you is greater than the one who is in the world (1 John 4:4)! Uproot the root of destruction and mediocrity in your life by quitting the life in the flesh for life in the spirit. Choose to be led by the Holy Spirit. Living a new life in Christ sets a man free from the law of sin and death that limits potentials and subject to the control of Satan (Eph.2: 1-3).
Like in real life, aircraft never crashes from one single issue; it is always a combination of issues that lead to an unavoidable crash. One crash might have been caused by the combination of a mechanical problem, bad weather and pilot error. If any one of these problems is missing, a crash might not happen. So the same way fatigue, poor weather, bad

standard of training or mechanical issues can singularly or jointly cause an accident, the same way any of the human vices, singularly or jointly can team up to wreck a human potential and existence. It is in your advantage to uproot sin and all types of vices operating in your life.

## Keep soaring with explosive potentials

*But the fruit of the Spirit is love, joy, peace, longsuffering, gentleness, goodness, faith, 23 Meekness, temperance: against such there is no law. 24 And they that are Christ's have crucified the flesh with the affections and lusts. 25 If we live in the Spirit, let us also walk in the Spirit. Gal 5:22-25*

*There is therefore now no condemnation to them which are in Christ Jesus, who walk not after the flesh, but after the Spirit. 8 For the law of the Spirit of life in Christ Jesus hath made me free from the law of sin and death. Rom 8:1-2*

There is no more condemnation to "them"!
To whom? To those who are in Christ Jesus, who no longer walk after the things of the flesh but after the things of the spirit.
Such has been set free from every evil limitation that restrains people of the flesh from living a life of excellence, legacy and greatness.
A Christian has two natures. The new life which he received when he accepted Jesus Christ as his Lord and Saviour, and the old sinful nature called "the flesh" in which he was living before.
The old nature is characterized by sinful desires which keep a man low and abased while the new nature that lifts a man's spirit is controlled by the Holy Spirit. When we become believers, our old nature neither gets destroyed nor changed. It requires conscious efforts to rid ourselves of the sinful nature. Those who are in Christ Jesus have to consciously take steps to sacrifice the flesh and commit to the transformation of their souls. Such have to discard their old human nature of living in selfishness and evil and follow the leadership of the Holy Spirit into a new life awaiting us in Christ. Living on top is a possibility now because of the spirit of the Lord living in you. Growing in the fruits of the spirit is also possible- and that is the fruit that is behind the exploits achieved by all the great men in the Bible. You now share the same spirit of the Lord with all the co-heirs of the kingdom of God, and now you can join hands together God's corporate purpose for humanity.

## Soar with the power of the Holy Spirit

When you focus on doing the things God likes, you are not alone, because God gave us His Spirit, which stands by us. He is our helper. We like to think that He is only our helper in giving us what we want, but He is more than that. He is our helper in teaching us to fly.

He is our Flying Instructor. The Holy Spirit helps us to understand the word of God and align our lives to the direction of the Lord.

Once you have learnt the victorious steps of living in the Lord keep soaring and never stop. Once you begin to experience victory in your new life, keep flying. No pilot would get the idea to put off the engine, just because the aeroplane is operating well. In the same way, we shouldn't get the idea, when we live in the Spirit and our life goes on well, to stop living a heavenly life.

If we do that, our aeroplane will nose dive and crash.

You can be flying successfully for the last half a century, but as soon you stop and fall back into your old nature, the law of sin and death will take over and you will crash. As long as we live in this world, we will always have the remnants of the old nature relegated within us. This nature cannot be eliminated, but it can become ineffective when we starve it and feed well our new nature with the word of God and life of the spirit. Like a soaring aeroplane, our enormous responsibility is to actively engage the law of lift by living under the law of the spirit by faith!

To remain passive or inactive in the Lord is a dangerous situation. Once you have learnt the victorious steps of flying in the Lord, keep soaring. Don't stop! To keep enjoying freedom from the sinking force of sin and death, you need to actively apply the heavenly laws of the Spirit of life in Christ Jesus. That is the only way to keep soaring in life.

---

> **Like a soaring aeroplane, our enormous responsibility is to actively engage the law of lift by living under the law of the spirit by faith!**
> **To remain passive or inactive in the Lord is a dangerous situation.**
> **Once you have learnt the victorious steps of flying in the Lord, keep soaring. Don't stop!**

## PRINCIPLES FOR PROTECTING YOUR POTENTIAL

1) God does not revoke potential from a person so long the person remains alive. Only the death of a man can terminate his potential.

2) The termination of potential is the death of a purpose.

3) Every seed is greatly affected by its environment.

4) The enemy, in a bid to ruin you will first try to uproot you from your right environment.

5) Sometimes, if the enemy finds it difficult to uproot you from a fertile place, he will resort to attacking your character so that he can corrupt your personality.

6) The enemy's ultimate goal for contaminating your potential is to terminate your life purpose.

7) The war against your potentials is more than a battle for your existence; it is an attack against God's hidden treasures inside of you and a battle against the lives of other people connected to you.

8) The "flesh" is our natural human nature with a natural tendency to sin.

9) Every believer is a seed of God. He is an eagle born to soar.

10) A Christian has two natures. The new life which he received when he accepted Jesus Christ as his Lord and Saviour, and the old sinful nature called "the flesh" in which he was living before.

11) When you focus on doing the things God likes, you are not alone, for the Holy Spirit stands with you.

12) To remain passive or inactive in the Lord is a dangerous situation.

## CHAPTER 11: EXERCISING DOMINION MANDATE

*And God blessed them, and God said unto them, Be fruitful, and multiply, and replenish the earth, and subdue it: and have dominion over the fish of the sea, and over the fowl of the air, and over every living thing that moveth upon the earth. Gen 1:28*

Your life has been specially set up as a stage for you to exercise your dominion mandate successfully. The foundation for your success is solid – it is the blessing of God!
God's plan for you and other kingdom citizens is to enjoy a reign of dominion. And because the sky is big enough for every eagle to sow, someone's reign of dominion is no challenge for another reign.
Every son of God however needs to observe the rules of the kingdom. Freedom without law breeds anarchy.
There cannot be freedom without law. Every liberty is insured by the law that serves as umpire between all stakeholders. There are also kingdom laws to observe to reign in your God-given platform and domain.

### The Rule of the Game

*I am the vine, ye are the branches: He that abideth in me, and I in him, the same bringeth forth much fruit: for without me ye can do nothing.* **John 15:5**

The authority to have dominion is not by human power or might but by the power of the Holy Spirit of the Lord.
Many people may like to carry out the dominion mandate of God in their lives without having any relationship with God, the Mandator. That is impossible. Without Him, the Source, you can do nothing!
So then it does not depend on the man who wills or the man who runs, but on God who has mercy (Romans 9:16 NASB)
God's law of potential demands an intimate connection between God - the Source of the mandate (the Mandator) and you - the executor of the mandate (the mandatory).

### The strength of your mandate

a)   Your Mandator is unretrenchable and un-removable!
The importance of a mandator can never be overemphasised in the execution of a mandate. The mandate is a written authorization by a 'mandator' to another (the 'mandatary') to take a certain course of action.

Normally revocable until executed, a mandate is automatically terminated on the bankruptcy, incapacitation, removal from office, or death of the mandator.[5] The special thing about your mandate is that it is from God. Your mandate is as powerful as your Mandator - irrevocable!

b)   Your Mandate is irrevocable
You see, your mandate is as irrevocable as your Mandator.
Since no one can remove God from office, your dominion mandate is irrevocable. Since God is un-terminable, your mandate to have dominion is irretrievable. Your Mandator is the omniscient, omnipresent and omnipotent God. The power of the dominion mandate is based on the eternal existence of the Mandator. Since God is alive forever, His mandate like Him is irrevocable.

c)   Your potential is irrevocable
Your potential is as powerful and irrevocable as your Source – God!
For God's gifts and his call can never be withdrawn. (Romans 11:29). The gifts, the favour, the anointing, the blessings, the honour which the Lord has given you are irrevocable. Nobody can steal them, nor can you ever lose them, nor does God take them away. The devil can only delay but cannot deny you what God designated for you. Nothing can destroy your potential but yourself. Stop ignoring your potential. Use it!

d)   The power to achieve your potential is of the Lord!
The Source of a product determines the potential of such a product. Just like its maker determines the power of a Mercedes Benz car has God, your Maker, determines your potential.
You carry inside of you God-Type of potential!
Greater is He that is in you than he that is in the world.
The Bible teaches that God spoke to the source when creating new objects. God spoke to the soil to create plants (Genesis 1:11-12). He spoke to the sea to create fish (Gen 1:20-21).
When it was the turn to create man, He spoke to Himself (Gen 1:26). The power to maintain your life is not in you but your Maker.

e)   The maintenance of a creature is by its source.

---

[5] http://www.businessdictionary.com/definition/mandate.html

Faithful is the Lord that calls you and who also will do what He calls you to do through you (1 Thess.5:24). The power to fulfil your potential is that of the Lord. You only need to connect to Him.
All living things die once they are detached from their source.
Adam died (spiritually) as soon as he fell away from God.
Common to great men who make the best of their potentials is the awareness of the importance of God in their lives. They made Him their priorities. They knew only he would decide if their lives would be considered successful or not. They knew only God could determine where they spend their eternity. The Psalmist said, "If I go up to heaven, you are there. If I make my bed in hell, you are there (Psalm 139:8)."
When creatures die, they return to the source from where they are created. When a man dies too, he returns to his Maker.
All the revelations above should empower you with a great passion not only to maximize your potentials but to do it with God by your side. The first man that ever lived started life with the blessing of the Lord. Everyone who wants to maximize his potential should do the same.

f) Leadership is about having dominion over your area of gifting.
God will not command you to do what He has not equipped you to do. God's instruction to man to have dominion over his environment is proof that God has deposited sufficient potential in every human being to do just that. It is left for individuals to take the responsibility to discover, develop and deploy fully personal talent.
It is your responsibility to unlock your potential, develop it and serve it! You are simply an author writing the scripts of your own life, and at the end of the day, you will have nobody or situation to blame for the result. That is the way to have dominion.
Many are still getting the concept of leadership wrong.

i. No man is expected to have dominion over another man.
   A man is only allowed to have a significant influence in his area of developed potential and expertise. The basis of the relationship between humanity is unity, not force. It is cooperation, not competition. Humanity is created to complement each other and not to oppress or discriminate against each other. What a great joy it brings when humanity can co-operate together (Psalm 133:1-3.) Human unity is what makes miracles happen. We are all co-heir with Christ, and we are only expected to support, mentor, encourage and

bring the best out of each other as we operate mutual dominion over plants and animals and our general environments.

ii. No situation is expected to have dominion over mankind. That is why man can treat sickness and surmount life challenges. There is no limit to what a man can achieve if he will resolutely pursue it.

iii. No environment is created to have dominion over mankind. That is why man can climb the highest of mountains regardless of the risk involved. We human beings experience pains when things (money, conditions, environments, fame) or people dominate us. This is contrary to God's plan of humans having dominion over their environment and circumstances.

## Executing Your Dominion Mandate

*And God blessed them, and God said unto them, Be fruitful, and multiply, and replenish the earth, and subdue it: and have dominion over the fish of the sea, and over the fowl of the air, and over every living thing that moveth upon the earth.* **Gen 1:28**

God's purpose for man is to have dominion on earth.
What God spoke to Abram, He spoke to us all.
All the believers have the mutual mandate to bring Kingdom Dominion on earth as Ambassadors of Christ. No matter who you are, you have been given the mandate to achieve dominion in an area.
Dominion is God's idea. Don't allow false humility to ruin you.
There is a place of influence for everyman including you!
Dominion mandates require taking four steps

- be fruitful
- multiply
- replenish the earth &
- subdue the earth

## 1) Be fruitful
To be fruitful, a seed needs to grow up into a tree that can replicate the same seed. Being fruitful is a test of faithfulness to becoming yourself. To be fruitful means, "reveal yourself through the maturity process".

You need to be faithful to the process of growth to bring out the good quality of you. You need to be faithful to the purpose of your existence. A mango seed can only become mango, and an orange tree can only become orange. You are to become what you are designed to be!
The purpose of any self-development you engage in is to become yourself, not another person. Be faithful to your design. Stop copying. Bible calls us only to be an imitator of good people. Imitate the great principles in their lives and apply it to make yours a better one.
In the parable of the talent given by Jesus Christ, the man with one talent was not fruitful because he chose to engage in the losing game of comparison. He ignored his seed leaving it the same while other stewards traded with their gifts and skills. He remained as God created him.
That is retardation resulting from in action.
No parent is happy with a retarded kid that will not grow.
That steward did not live. He just occupied space!
What is the profit of a faithful tree that never produces any fruit?
Jesus Christ cursed such a type in the Bible (Mark 11:12-21).
God expects his creatures to be faithful as much as they are fruitful.
To be fruitful demands that you develop your potential to fulfil your purpose. Until a seed works out the potential inside it through sacrificial labour, it abides alone. It lives unfruitful.
No wonder the Master (God) called the servant with one talent, lazy.
He refused to labour to release the power inside his potential.
He refused to process his potential.

## Seven principles of fruitfulness

(1) God is the source of all seeds (potential). Every manufacturer builds the potential into his product. The potential to fulfil God's dominion mandate is deposited in every man as a seed.
(2) God has empowered all his creatures to be fruitful. Blessing means the supernatural enablement to become what you are created to be. God blessed the first man even before giving him the mandate (Gen.1:28).
(3) God's instruction "Be" is no suggestion. You're commanded by your Maker to convert the seed you carry into fruits). It is therefore natural for man to be fruitful. God invested a lot in man, put his spirit on him and expects him to bear fruits. Every believer has the mandate to be fruitful.

(4) God has no plan for you to be sterile, barren, infertile or suffer any miscarriage. Unproductivity and unfruitfulness is proof of a curse and it is not of the Lord. God blessed the first man and the blessing of the Lord makes rich and He adds no sorrow to it (Proverbs10:22).

(5) Faithfulness is the source of fruitfulness. It is required in steward to be found faithful (1 Cor.4:2). To one he gave five talents,[b] to another two, to another one, to each according to his ability. Then he went away. (Matt.25:15). Fruitfulness demands taking responsibility!

i. Taking the responsibility to develop your potential to perfection is proof of faithfulness (to your Maker).

ii. Your faithfulness in developing your potential (spirit, body and soul) is a significant determinant of your productivity in life.

iii. Fruitfulness is a reward of faithfulness. By their fruits, you shall know them. Every product is a fruit of someone's potential development. Your fruits make known your labour. Everyone should develop potential enough to add high values to his or her generation.

(6) Your productivity affects your life's reward. Do you see a man that is diligent in his business? He shall stand before kings; he shall not stand before mean men (Prov. 22:29).

(7) Your Maker will judge the fruitfulness of your life in terms of His purpose (not yours). Your potentials are given to you to help you fulfil life purpose. How many needs are you meeting?
How many problems are you solving? Are you fruitful?

**Seven Major Areas of fruitfulness**

Fruitfulness is more than having fruits of labour or fruits of the womb; it includes prosperity in every area of life.

**(1) Fruits from talents**

We are all gifted and talented. You can create something out of the deposits in your life. You are a natural solution provider, filled with potentials to solve life challenges. You can be a footballer, a cook, a boxer, or a good employee. Whatever you do, "Johnny be good!"

**(2) Fruits of the womb**

God intends man to continue to procreate to maintain human circulation on earth. It is one of the areas of taking dominion of the earth. Children are a heritage of the LORD: and the fruit of the womb is his reward (Psalm 127:3).

### (3) Fruits of the thought
These are products from human ideas. Many of the things we do in life are the products of our thoughts. That is why God wants us to renew our minds so that we shall be creating great products from a heart that honours, love and glorify God ( Prov. 23:7; Rom.12:2). The major wealth of any nation remains the collective intelligence of her citizen.

### (4) Fruits of the mouth
The words we speak are fruits of our mouth, and they come out of what we deposit in our heart. To produce good, life-giving words, we need to invest quality time in studying and meditating the words of God (Prov. 18:20-21; Luke 6:45, Matt.12.34).

### (5) Fruits of the hands
Labour is the fruits of a man's hand. It is what exhibits your developed potentials. Labour is God's way of granting man prosperity (Psalm 1:3, Deut. 8:18, Prov. 31:31). All hard work brings a profit, but mere talk leads only to poverty.(Prov.14:23).

### (6) Fruits of the spirit
God also expects us to produce ethical and moral values (character). *But the fruit of the Spirit is love, joy, peace, longsuffering, gentleness, goodness, faith, 23 meekness, temperance: against such there is no law (Gal 5:22-23).*
It was the fruits of the spirit that Pharaoh saw in Joseph that made him promote him from a prisoner to prime minister (Gen 41:37-38).

### (7) Fruits of the kingdom
The fruit of the righteous is a tree of life, and the wise one saves lives. (Prov.11:30). We are not good Christians and disciples of Jesus Christ if we are not bringing fruits of the lost souls into the kingdom of God. No matter other fruits we bear, if we are not bearing fruits according to our kinds, we are barren (Gen. 1:11-27).

## You have been empowered by God to be fruitful!

*The righteous will flourish like a palm tree, they will grow like a cedar of Lebanon; 13 planted in the house of the LORD, they will flourish in the courts of our God. 14 They will still bear fruit in old age, they will stay fresh and green, 15 proclaiming, "The LORD is upright; he is my Rock, and there is no wickedness in him." Psalm 92:12(NIV)*

Let the truth of God's words set you free.
Be fruitful is not a promise, it is an instruction, a commission.
God has empowered you. Delay of your dream is no denial.
Be fruitful in your body, mind, soul and all undertakings.

## Unfruitful life attracts God's wrath

Prayer cannot substitute your potential development. Work it out!
Faith without work is dead.
Jesus Christ cursed the unproductive olive tree (Matt. 21:19).
The Master (God) cursed the unproductive steward (Matt. 25:26-28).
Do not be deceived, God cannot be mocked, whatever a man sows, same shall he reap (Galatians 6:7).

## 2) Multiply

*24 And God said, "Let the earth bring forth living creatures according to their kinds: livestock, land crawlers, and wild animals according to their kinds." And it was so. 25 God made the beasts of the earth according to their kinds, the livestock according to their kinds, and everything that crawls upon the earth according to its kind. And God saw that it was good. 26 Then God said, "Let Us make man in Our image, after Our likeness, to rule over the fish of the sea and the birds of the air, over the livestock, and over all the earth itself and every creature that crawls upon it." Genesis 1:24.26*

Multiplication talks about the duplication of your gifts or personalities in the lives of others. To multiply means to increase and reproduce more of your fruits in great quantity. Many people stop at being fruitful. They stopped before reaching the place of abundance in the Lord.
To multiply, a fruitful tree needs to reproduce its fruits to reap many other trees. Many selfish and self-centred people cannot reach this stage. They are satisfied with being fruitful enough to cater for their families.

However, God's purpose of blessing us is to turn us into a great blessing to many others (Genesis 12.2-3).

Only mature believers are permitted to reach the stage of multiplication because it can be very dangerous for immature people. That should remind you of the rich fool who lost his life because of greed (Luke 12:13-21). He died from the erosion of Tsunamis blessing for trying to hoard in his reservoir the sea of God's blessing.

God's process hardly permits immature children or anything to multiply. That is because the act of multiplication is an act of maturity. You need maturity to multiply in the kingdom of God. You need the maturity to let your God-given resources go back to the work of God (Luke 12:21). Only a man who is comfortable with himself can add value to others. Only a man that is confident in his calling can duplicate himself in others. Only mature people can share principles, ideas and revelations that make them who they are trusting God for continuous increase.

It is not enough to be yourself or reproduce physical children. God also expects you to raise people of your kind. You are expected to multiply yourself in others, by influencing them to share your faith, principles and values in their lives. You are expected to influence your dependents, friends, associates, workers, employers' etcetera

## The Principles of multiplication (Matt. 25:14-20)

1) We are all stewards
   Man is the manager of God's resources on earth.
   It is required that every steward be found faithful (1 Cor. 4:2).
   Be faithful in bringing out who you are created to be by investing in your potentials. Every man shares in the Adamic mandate to manage the earth. We all have an area in life where we are created to dominate for the glory of the Lord. God didn't allow rain to fall on earth at the beginning of creation because there was no man to work the ground. God permits no increase where there are no managers (Gen 2:5,15).

2) We are expected to be effective stewards
   To be effective steward requires locating your area of influence and competence (Matt.25:15). Running an effective business begins with understanding your manufacturer's mindset for your existence. The Master in Jesus parable gave each steward according to their several abilities. Finding the problem that you are created to solve is your key to the wealthy place. You are not designed to solve every problem.

3) All stewards are required to hone their skills
   The stewards with five and two talents immediately began to invest in their gifts (Matt.25:16-18). The steward with one talent decided to hide his potential. Faithfulness is about developing your potential to fruitfulness. All you have to do is take the step of faith.

4) To multiply requires good management of your fruits (resources)
   The steward with five talents made another five talents and the steward with two talents made another two talents (Matt.25: 20-23).
   You cannot multiply any fruit or product until the seed grew to a tree that can bear fruits. To multiply is about choosing between eating your fruits now or postponing compensation till a later day. It is a choice between enjoying instant reward or postponing gratification. To multiply requires saving your best fruits for tomorrow.

5) Mismanagement attracts lack
   While proper management attracts prosperity to the first two stewards, mismanagement attracted lack to the lazy steward (Matt.25:24-26).
   God demands increase (fruitfulness and multiplication) from all His stewards. If you cannot account for the resources you have now, God will not increase you with more. God gives you more of what you can manage not what you pray for. Until you can account for what you are given, God will not give you more.
   Every steward needs to put an order in personal life.
   God will not allow growth and multiplication where there is no proper management (fruitfulness).
   You need to be fruitful before you can multiply.

6) The prosperity of your business is a product of your faithful work
   Whatsoever he does shall prosper (Psalm 1:3) not whatsoever he hopes or thinks! God expects us to put to work our potentials be it much or little. Whoever can be trusted with very little can also be trusted with much, and whoever is dishonest with very little will also be dishonest with much. And if you are untrustworthy about worldly wealth, who will trust you with the true riches of heaven (Lk. 16:10-11)?
   We cheat ourselves out of prosperity wherever we fail to work very hard on developing our potentials by honing our skills.

7) Multiplication is a product of investment
You can only multiply what you give out. God gives the seed out to both the eater and the sower but only rewards the seeds sowed (2. Cor.9:10). God will always give you seed and leave you the responsibility of deciding to eat or to sow.
Multiplication is however a reward for investment not for the consumption of your resources. Give and it shall be given to you. A good measure, pressed down, shaken together and running over, will be poured into your lap. For with the measure you use, it will be measured to you (Luke 6:38). Becoming rich and wealthy goes beyond just earning a salary. Begin to invest with your resources.

## 3) Replenish

Replenish means to fill and make full or complete again.
Replenish was used seven times in the Bible and at all time it means to fill (Gen.1:28; Gen. 9:1; Isa 2:6; Jer. 31:25; Isa 23:2; Ez26:2; Ez. 27:25). God's original plan for man is to fill the earth with His glory. God had sent man, not angels on that mission to fill the earth with His glory!
Our goal is to bring His kingdom down on earth as it is in heaven.
We are to do His will on earth as it is in Heaven.
Christianity is more than serving the Lord inside the Church.
It's about God filling the earth with His glory through you!
God's plan is to prepare us within the church and send us back to the world to fill the earth with His glory. Today we are called to disciple both our children and all God's people, so the earth might be filled with redeemed image-bearers who will wisely manifest the Lord's sovereign holiness in their work, area of influence etc.
The kingdom of God is everywhere and the church is the custodian. The Church must spread the influence of the kingdom of God everywhere before the second coming of the Lord Jesus Christ.
Your profession, career, business, trade or calling is a platform to shine and to extend God's glory to the world.

**Principles of replenishment (Matt. 25:14-20)**

a) You social task is to fill your domain with your gifted ideas and invention (distribute & market).

Distribution is a major key in wealth creation. Distribute your products and services widely and use them to replenish wherever lacks and problems have created a need. The internet has given all the ability to distribute products all over the world and serve God's purpose.

**b)** Your spiritual mission is to fill the earth with the gospel of Christ And Jesus came and spake unto them, saying, All power is given unto me in heaven and the earth. Go ye therefore, and teach all nations, baptizing them in the name of the Father, and of the Son, and the Holy Ghost: Teaching them to observe all things whatsoever I have commanded you: and, lo, I am with you alway, even unto the end of the world. Amen" (Matthew 28:18-20). The market place is your pulpit to win souls as an ambassador of Christ with the mandate to restore humanity to the Lord (2 Cor. 5:17-20; Eph. 6:10-15).

c) You are to fill the earth with God's glory by resisting the power of darkness in your environment (Spiritual warfare)

All believers are called to wage warfare against the kingdom of darkness. We are the light of the world. Jesus Himself said to us, "Behold, I have given you authority to tread on serpents and scorpions, and over all the power of the enemy, and nothing shall hurt you (Luke 10:19).

In another place the Lord said, "And these signs shall follow them that believe; In my name shall they cast out devils; they shall speak with new tongues; 18 They shall take up serpents; and if they drink any deadly thing, it shall not hurt them; they shall lay hands on the sick, and they shall recover (Mk 16:17-18)."

## 4) Subdue (Bring under control)

Subdue" emphasizes human environmental stewardship part of the dominion mandate. By this, I mean that the dominion mandate has two major parts to it. One is for humanity to be fruitful and to multiply. The other is for man to enhance the fruitfulness of the earth.

That means to cultivate our environments and care for other creation! Jesus Christ had made the ultimate sacrifice not only to restore man to God but also to restore the earth to its old glory.

His thorny crown broke the curse upon the earth.

Jesus' redemptive work, therefore covers both man and the earth.

## PRINCIPLES FOR EXERCISING DOMINION MANDATE

1) Freedom without law breeds anarchy.

2) The authority to have dominion is not by human power or might but by the power of the Holy Spirit of the Lord.

3) Your Mandator is un-retrenchable and un-removable!

4) Your mandate is as irrevocable as your Mandator.

5) Your potential is as powerful as your Source – God!

6) No man is expected to have dominion over another man.

7) No situation is expected to have dominion over mankind

8) No environment is created to have dominion over mankind

9) God's purpose for man is to have dominion on earth.

10) Man is the manager of God's resources on earth.

11) Being a Christian carries greater responsibility than just going to church to worship on Sunday; we have the duty to influence the world and its system with the principles of the kingdom of God.

12) God's purpose for blessing you is to make you a blessing to others.

## CHAPTER 12: ENVIRONMENTAL STEWARDSHIP

*The LORD God took the man and put him in the Garden of Eden to work it and take care of it. Genesis 2:15*

To subdue the earth is one of God's primary mandates to mankind as a way of exercising dominion on earth. The topic of environmental stewardship is so vast and very relevant to the generation that I will like to devote a whole chapter to it. Right from the time of Adam, the first man that God placed in the Garden of Eden, God's instruction was for man, "to work it and take care of it." By keeping the Garden, the Bible is referring to human responsibility to take care of all of God's Creation.

As God protects humanity, so does He expects a man to keep and protect other Creation. In the Old Testament laws, for instance, the children of Israel were instructed to give rest to animals and also to the farming lands on Sabbath, same like humans (Exodus 20:8-11).

God did not only bless man to be fruitful, He blesses all His creatures and as the image of God on earth, it remains man's responsibility not to destroy the animal and sea lives that God has blessed him with.

Like Noah, we all need to take animals preservation very serious. The same way Noah prevented God's creatures from extinction are we expected to protect, provide and preserve the creatures.

Bad human stewardship of our environment has led to global warming and all other environmental ills. Though nature is given to bless man, it might still bring adverse consequence on us if we do not treat it right.

Definitions website defines subdue as "to bring under; to conquer by force or the exertion of superior power, and bring into permanent subjection; to reduce under dominion; to vanquish.".[6]

God's instrument to restore the earth remains the man.

As soon as we receive Christ, the King of glory into our heart, we accept the responsibility to carry out the dominion mandates. That explains why man can never stop experimenting with technology.

We have the urge to subdue our environment by every means possible. We manufacture cars, airplanes, ships just to subdue our environments. No mountain is too high or a sea too deep to subdue for the man! No generation has achieved technological advancement like ours.

---

[6] https://www.definitions.net/definition/subdue

None had ever threatened the continuity of earth like we also do.
We have created dangerous problems for our environment.
We live daily under the threat of nuclear energy warfare, atomic waste, environmental disaster, ozone depletion, global warming, deforestation, extinction of species- all these are increasing proofs that we're losing control over the environment we are meant to safeguard and protect.
We are called to reflect the moral character of God in subduing the earth. God never ravages or exploits what He rules, but rather reigns in justice and kindness" He saw darkness and created the light.
Subduing the earth is more than climbing mountains and tapping sea currents for electricity generation. God also has a plan for us to protect the earth. There is a fine line between using earthly resources in a responsible manner and exploitation of those resources in a way that is harmful to the rest of humanity or the animal kingdom.

## Principles guiding the subduement of the earth

### 1. Responsible use of earth's resources

As God's agents on earth, man is called to use carefully, effectively and profitably the earth natural resources – soil, water, land, energy, marine and ocean, minerals, animals, plants and even human resources without harming or polluting the environment.
We are called to rule the earth and not to ruin it.
In the Genesis 2:15 account of creation, Adam is said to have been placed in the Garden "to till it and keep it"= "take care of," "guard," or "watch over" the garden. A caretaker protects and not destroys!
We are to irresponsibly enjoy life resources without harming the animal kingdom and decimate our environment. We have the responsibility to feed our ever increasing population without damaging the environment.

### 2. Control of 'natural' disasters

Mankind is called to control natural disasters like earthquakes, tsunamis and the eruption of volcanoes. It is our responsibility to develop the capacity to accurately forecast these dangerous events to minimize their impact. We are to monitor and mitigate the harmful effects of hazardous weather particularly hurricanes, floods and droughts. Every government should proactively protect her populace from a natural disaster.
Part of the indices to measure a state's development is to watch their preparation- structures and strategies- against natural disasters.

If nothing tangible exists, such a state is a dangerous state and the government a worthless one for the first disaster to come might wipe out the entire population with her history.

A responsible society plans to protect her people from the unforeseen natural disaster. They do not wait for accidents and tragedy to strike before running around futilely and senselessly. Science and technology continue to develop high potentials to manage our environment. With it comes the increasing hope that we may learn how to control earthquakes and other natural disasters that are presently beyond human control.

3. **Control of domesticated and wild animals**

God has blessed humanity with the rich animal kingdom.
God has also placed that animal kingdom under the dominion of humankind. It is our responsibility to preserve our animal kingdom. Human mismanagement has led to the disappearance of many species. It remains our corporate duty to protect the remaining threatened species. That includes preserving extinct animals and threatened wild lives. Animal poaching should also be discouraged so that we can preserve them for other generations to meet.

4. **Protect the ocean and sea resources**

Humankind must protect sea life, prevent water pollution and preserve fish stocks. Our environment mismanagement has continued to ruin the sea life. Human waste has found its way to the ocean where it is harming sea animals. Hazardous plastic wastes have been found inside animals or covering their body, causing death and accidents of various types.

5. **Preserve agricultural lifestyles**

It remains human responsibility to adequately care for the diversity of plant-life and rain-forests and help to cure diseases in plants and our other agricultural products, so we do not pass it over to the consumers or our environment. Finding more efficient ways of growing food to feed an expanding population without destroying the land is good management. Israel had thought the world that it is possible to make the best of every environment by turning the desert land to a food basket that is fielding the world. Israel being a small country has vast areas of the country (at least 1/3) as a desert. Since Israel is surrounded by unfriendly neighbours' who threaten to destroy the land with profound food shortages, the land as survival strategy had to intensify technological advancement to improve her agricultural life. Today, anybody travelling through Israel's deserts is sure to see the tens of thousands of palm trees producing dates by the tons – all out of the harsh desert. Since an Israeli water engineer, Simcha Blass, revolutionized the concept of drip irrigation, agriculture has become a great source of income for the nation and drip irrigation technology has become a large Israeli industry that has been helping nations of the world suffering from infertile land to feed their people.

6. **Disease control**
Man has the responsibility to develop drugs and explore natural cures to eliminate the diseases that plague mankind and the animal kingdom. Healthily preserving the world for human existence is a priority for us all. While to the credit of science, some diseases like malaria, leprosy, smallpox and tuberculosis have been wholly, partly or largely eliminated we are faced with new challenges such as HIV and AIDS.

7. **Space monitoring**
Man has a duty also to control potential disasters from space.
It is important to monitor bodies that could have disastrous results and having a plan to prevent or deal with such an event.

8. **Social-political control**
Mankind needs to work together to eradicate greed, injustice, poverty, conflict, war and any other thing that hinder human socio-political progress and general wellbeing. Though no man is created to have dominion or to oppress another man, we can all still influence each other positively in our areas of gifting. When you use well your potentials, it will serve as an influential socio-political platform to lead other people. Finding ways of ensuring that everyone benefits in a fair and just society must be the pursuits of all followers of Christ. Though the world can feed all her citizens, poor leadership still make sure that people are dying of hunger every day. The United Nations are yet to take it as a serious priority to offer a standard of living to every citizen on earth. We all have it as a corporate duty to eliminate sickness, poverty, famine and anything that might ridicule and put to shame man- the image of God on earth.

9. **Environmental control**
Finding a way to use nuclear energy (particularly nuclear fusion) without pollution for us now and in future generations. Using the laws of physics to our advantage such as has been done with electricity, electromagnetic waves (radio waves etc.) and electronics (computers, communication etc.)

In case you have been wondering why some environmental conscious companies led by unbelievers have been making billions yearly, you have the answer now. They are being rewarded for pursuing godly goals of subduing the earth. Every time you obey God's instruction, a divinely set system rewards your efforts. It does not matter who applies the principles of the Lord, such principles will deliver a blessing.

## Which mountain are you taking over?

*Now therefore give me this mountain, whereof the Lord spake in that day; for thou heardest in that day how the Anakims were there, and that the cities were great and fenced: if so be the Lord will be with me, then I shall be able to drive them out, as the Lord said. Joshua 14:12*

Being a Christian carries greater responsibility than just going to church. We are to influence the world with the principles of God's kingdom . We are alive to bring His kingdom on earth as it is in heaven.
In 1975, Bill Bright, founder of Campus Crusade and Loren Cunningham, founder of Youth With A Mission (YWAM), developed a world-changing strategy, called the seven mountains.
They believe that believers can bring godly change to a nation by influencing with the principles of God the seven major spheres, or mountains of societal influence. The seven spheres they mentioned are:

(1) **Religion**: With a plethora of categorized religions around the world, it's the Church's responsibility to reach the lost with the love and Gospel of Jesus Christ, and expand the Kingdom in ministerial efforts, both nationally and internationally.

(2) **Family**: Family is suffering abuse, homosexual marriage, pornography, and other great dysfunctions. God wants to bring healing to marriages and relationships within families and maintain a moral foundation for children through the efforts of caring believers.

(3) **Education**: The havoc in our society is connected to the moral depravity that our students are plunged into as the educational system. Gone were the days when Bible teaching was part and parcel of education. Today our learning institutions are filled with liberal ideologies, atheistic teaching and postmodern principles that are often false, biased and non-scriptural. We need courageous believers who

can re-introduce biblical truth and values back into our educational system. That will be a major step to restore moral values to society.

(4) **Government**: Under the guise of "separation of church and state," many pressure groups have sought to remove anything related to God or Christianity from the governmental and educational systems of their land. The church needs to train righteous and courageous believers to join political organisations so that they can restore righteousness into the arena of power. "Righteousness exalts a nation, but sin is a reproach to any people (Proverbs 14:34)."

(5) **Media**: Societal morality has come to an all-time low level because the owners of media houses are mostly non-believers that make money out of the fraudulent lifestyle their Media are fostering on people. The media has the potential to sway popular opinion and lifestyle. There is an increasing need for believers to take over and transform the Media Mountain (Internet, radio, TV news stations, newspapers etcetera).

(6) **Arts & Entertainment**: some of the most influential forces shaping our al values and standards are found in the Music, filmmaking, television, social media and performing arts, etcetera. Most of the population take their role models from this mountain than from the church so if it is important for the church to see lives transformed, it needs to leave the four walls of the church and invade the mountain of entertainment. The body of Christ needs powerful, righteous men and women who are not afraid to take their God-given talent into the arts and entertainment arenas.

(7) **Business**: The ability to make wealth is from the Lord (Deut.8:18, Isa 48:17, Prov.10:22). The church must be involved in the economic welfare of the members by not just only empowering them to perform successfully, but also moulding their character. The mountain of business is prone to greed, corruption and covetousness. The Church has to train those who are called into the marketplace to provide leadership with integrity and honesty. Believers must influence the world by teaching win-win mentality as opposed the winner take it all greedy system that is ruining business everywhere.

**More Mountains:**

I have located many other mountains where believers can make a difference. These include among others:
- Science and technology
- Sports and recreation
- Communication and transportation
- Health

Whichever another mountain you may find, so long you have passion for it, it is your duty to take it over by bringing godly influence there.
Every believer has a Promised Land in the agenda of God for humanity. Your duty, like Caleb, is to locate and take over your mountain where you will reign and bring God glory.

## Time to give back

God's purpose for blessing you is to make you a blessing to others. Even as the Lord blesses you, it is your responsibility to bless your community, your environment, your nation and your generation.
Give back to your community and the next generation.
For some, it means starting a personal company or foundation that can help others. For another, it means finding a good company to work.
We cannot all do the same thing. We do not all carry the same potentials. We all however have our mountain where we are uniquely equipped to prevail. God has called all of us to find an area to subdue.
More than climbing the physical mountains, God has called us to manage the whole universe and all that is in it.
However to be able to give back to our environment and preserve it, we also need to subdue human nature. Greed, envy and fear produce injustice, poverty and conflict that have tremendously negative effects of upon the aim of subduing the Earth. With God's help, we can deal with greed and fear in our own lives. By living a life in the spirit, we can tame our flesh excesses and make the world a better place for everyone.
We are called to reflect the righteous character of God in subduing the earth. It is our corporate responsibility as mankind to protect the earth and make it a better place for every man, animal and plant. We can look after the earth in a responsible manner that will not destroy it for our children and us while enjoying its resources and potential. Subduing the Earth or bringing it under control requires responsible management. We are called to be God's environmental managers, not destroyers!

## PRINCIPLES OF ENVIRONMENTAL STEWARDSHIP

1) Being a Christian carries greater responsibility than just going to church to worship on Sunday; we have the duty to influence the world and its system with the principles of the kingdom of God.

2) Bad human stewardship of our environment has led to global warming and all other environmental ills.

3) To subdue the earth is one of God's major mandates to mankind as a way of exercising dominion on earth.

4) God's instrument to restore the earth remains the man.

5) As God's agents on earth, man is called to use carefully, effectively and profitably the earth natural resources.

6) Mankind is called to control natural disasters like earthquakes, tsunamis and the eruption of volcanoes.

7) Mankind has a duty to protect and preserve wild lives.

8) Mankind must protect sea life, prevent water pollution and preserve fish stocks.

9) It remains a human responsibility to adequately care for the diversity of plant-life and rain-forests and help to cure diseases in plants and our other agricultural products.

10) Man has the responsibility to develop drugs and explore natural cures to eliminate the diseases that plague mankind and animals.

11) Man has a duty also to control potential disasters from the space.

12) Mankind needs to work together to eradicate greed, injustice, war and any other socio-political injustice on earth.

## CHAPTER 13: BECOMING A PERSON OF VALUE

*"The illiterate of the 21st century will not be those who cannot read and write, but those who cannot learn, unlearn, and relearn." Alvin Toffler*

Your Maker already determines your true worth through the purpose that He created you to serve. You can however not pursue and fulfil your purpose until you first discover, develop and deploy your potentials. The essence of discovering, developing and deploying your potential is to become a person of value.
God created every man to be valuable to His kingdom by offering valuable services to God's creatures on earth.
You see, you are on earth on purpose to add values.
The language of the market place is that of value.
You are not paid for the hour you serve but for the value you add to people's lives per hour. That is why, though it is good to work hard on your job, it pays more to work harder on yourself.
It takes valuable labourer to offer valuable labour.
A man cannot give what he does not have!
Remaining relevant in the market place is a major challenge of the 21$^{st}$ century where the whole world has been reduced to a technological village where distances and geographical boundaries matter no more.
You now compete with workers and markets all over the world.
You need to be highly competitive and advanced to remain valuable in the market. Most of the countries now build their economies on offering goods and services to other nations. How can you stay relevant in such an interconnected marketplace or economy?
It is by making sure your service remains as relevant as you are.
You need to remain a person of value at all time.
You need to be more focus on being valuable than being successful.
What is considered to be successful today may become dead and irrelevant tomorrow. The only way to keep abreast of development is to remain a person of value. Make yourself more valuable than the present job.

*Try not to become a person of success, but rather a person of value" - Albert Einstein.*

Does Albert Einstein mean we should not pursue success? No!
Success is the achievement of a goal. We all need plans and goals and we all need to be successful if we will live a productive life. But just pursuing a goal successfully is not enough if it has no value behind it.

Being successful isn't always the hardest thing in the world, but doing it with a sense of value while holding to your value system.

Some people only keep their eyes on success, no matter how it comes. Some do not care if they lose their integrity and humanity in pursuits of success. Such people are unethical and very dangerous to humanity.

We all respect people who keep their sights on great values for corporate mankind even it cost them their comforts. Such selfless stewards end up both successful and good in the sight of the populace.

A good name is priceless and quite worthy than silver and gold!

Not all successful efforts lead to progress!

Some lead to the accumulation of stress.

We are not here to accumulate wealth and materials that have just temporal existence. The purpose of life is living a life of purpose.

We are created to add values to the world and the people inside it.

> **The essence of discovering, developing and deploying your potential is to become a person of value.**

## Putting a value on your life

Does your presence make a difference to others?

You are created on purpose to make a difference!

You are created as a solution provider who should add values unto other people's lives. You become significant to others only when you make a meaningful impact on their lives. You can only make a significant impact on others only when you foremost add values to your own life.

To achieve your purpose, you need to live on purpose.

You are not here to run a rat race and gather perishable materials.

You are rather here on Majesty's Assignment.

Your duty is to serve God's purpose, at your best, unto your generation.

Certain disciplines and practices make you valuable to the world.

### (1) Live on principles

A person of value is a principled person guided by moral values.

Your principles are the totality of your value system.

Becoming a person of value begins with being led by values.

You cannot really live until you have great values to live for. A valuable life is a life whose value to self and others outlives immediate gain.

The English Oxford Dictionary defines principle as a rule or belief governing one's behaviour. It's a personal philosophy determining how you process ideas and responds to the situation.

While our circumstances, conditions, challenges, connections and chemistry might affect our lives, social findings have confirmed that 80% of what surely happened to us in life is a product of our choice.

Personal philosophy puts our lives in order and makes our life choices and pursuits' predictable. That fact shows the importance of having principles (personal philosophy) for guiding our lives.

Everyone is held captive to the principles practiced in life. Our principles determine our behaviour, and our behaviours affect our destiny. Remember however that, while behaviour shows what we are outside (personality), character reveals what we are inside. Character is a product of our value system. Do you now see the connection I am making?

Your value system creates your character (who you are inside) while your character determines your behaviour (who you are outside).

The root of who you are is the principles that guide your life! Successful life is designed to operate on principles. No lasting greatness is made by assumptions and presumptions but by principles.

A life without principles is bound to fail.

Behind every greatness is the application of principles. Every great business, service or products follows a regular pattern and principles. Everyone can manifest blessing by applying the principles of blessing to life. Everyone can do exploits in life by choosing to apply principles of exploits in what is done. Living by principles help you leave behind great legacy than gross tragedy. Focus more on living life of principle than cheap success and popularity.

> **While our circumstances, conditions, challenges, connections and chemistry might affect our lives, social findings have confirmed that 80% of what surely happened to us in life is a product of our choice.**

### Set up your core values

A value system is a set of ideas that guide your personal behaviour. Your values determine your priorities in life. Your values are the core beliefs that shape who you are as a person, and how you live your life.

They determine the things you can do and cannot do. You cannot live on principles until you set up your personal value system.

When many options seem reasonable, it's helpful and comforting to rely on your values. By becoming aware of the values that are more important factors in your life, you can make a better choice in any situation. When your value is clear, making a decision and getting your priority right becomes very easy.

People asked me why I left my banking career as associate director for pastoring. It was a case of getting my value system right.

I know my purpose for existence and it is more than making money.

I consider my calling more important and quite valuable to others than sitting all week long behind my banking desk all in the name of making more money while many precious lives were needing my attention fizzle away. You can simply not substitute values for cheap success.

If you do that, no matter how many people consider you successful in your field, you will always feel empty and frustrated and will lack fulfilment in life. Living by principle boils down to identifying your life values and allowing them to direct your life.

Your value system determines who you are.

A man of lie is a liar, and a man of dignity is a priceless gem.

Your value system also determines the direction of your life.

Do you see a diligent man, he will stand before kings; he will not stand before obscure men (Prov.22:29). That also implies that your value system will significantly affect your career compensation.

Lastly, remain a man of impeccable character that can be depended on at all time. Some people gossip and slander others to get ahead of the pack. That will always boomerang in the long run. Being good to others is good business. You need to be so remarkable to become irreplaceable. Strive for personal excellence at all the time.

> **You can simply not substitute values for cheap success.**
> **If you do that, no matter how many people consider you successful in your field, you will always feel empty and frustrated and will lack fulfilment in life.**

**(2) Discover your uniqueness**

Celebrate your uniqueness because there is only one of you.
The greatest discovery in life is self-discovery.
A man's gift makes room for him, and brings him before great men(Prov. 18:16). Every man is gifted. Have you discovered yours?
Your gifts and potentials are directions to your life purpose so find it.
Although everyone on earth has a unique purpose, this does not mean that everyone is aware of his or her purpose. And where the purpose of a thing is not known, abuse and misuse are inevitable.
Without locating your destiny and purpose, your life becomes a sheer experiment - like playing football with no goal post. Quite frustrating!
Destiny in the other hand is not decided but discovered.
The discovery of your destiny is your duty and responsibility.
Your real life, in fact, begins the day you discover your destiny.
With it comes an understanding of our uniqueness as individuals.
King Solomon did not mention that a man's pedigree or degree make way for him. The ultimate way maker he discovered was a man's gift.
Every person is gifted. Every person has a potential which can be unlocked and used to obtain explosive results beyond our imagination.
A by-product of self-discovery is self-confidence. A self-confident man needs no external affirmation or confirmation to pursue his purpose.
The day you find what is worth dying for to live for is the day you begin to live. Once you discover your unique talent, devote yourself to its pursuits. If you are still employed or in school, start spending time to gather information and follow up developments in your field of interest.
It is the purpose that you devote your life into that makes a great difference between merely existing and living.

**Recognize and accept your difference**
It's your uniqueness that ultimately makes you valuable.
You are born an original so refuse to die as photo or carbon copy of another person. That is a fake copy of yourself.
You came to this world as an original so don't live or leave as a duplicate.
To be unique, you need to be yourself.
Everybody is meant to be "the" Principal Actor of his life.
To be authentic, you need to genuinely stick to your original purpose.
To be valuable, you need to be the best of yourself.
To remain relevant, you need to continue to improve yourself.
You have to progressively increase your service in quality and quantity until you dominate your area of influence. In other words, do not

measure your success next to someone else's or to their standards of what success should be. Measure them according to your best ability!

- **Identify your uniqueness.** It is your uniqueness that distinguishes you from others. To add values to others, you first need to recognize and celebrate your uniqueness.
  Your uniqueness makes you significant.
- **Recognize your difference.** It is what creates demands for your service. God purposefully made us different from one another. Being rare puts you in demand. Being common makes you cheap.
- **Explore your difference.** Your life was never meant to be like that of everyone else. You are created differently, equipped differently and positioned differently to achieve a unique purpose on earth.
- **Maximize your identity.** Your uniqueness is for your identity. Celebrate it. Your life is the greatest asset you own. Learn great principles from others to maximize your potential and make yourself a better person.

### (3) Invest in self - development

To remain a person of value demands that you continuously go through a process of developing yourself to serve your gift in the best way you can do so that you can remain relevant to your organisation.

Becoming a person of value is about breaking personal barriers and limits to become a better self. It is beyond competing with people or computers. It is about remaining relevant to the problems of the day and remaining a solution provider. You are to strive to remain a pacesetter and a game changer in your field as you continue a process of continuous self-appraisal, evaluation and rediscovery on how to bring progress to our common humanity.

No matter the challenges of the digital transformation of the economy, a person of value will continue to evolve and remain relevant to the market place. Even though one robot (Artificial Intelligence) may be able to do the work of 100 simple people, 100 robots cannot still do the work of one unique person of value.

**Prepare yourself**

*Declaring the end from the beginning, and from ancient times the things that are not yet done, saying, My counsel shall stand, and I will do all my pleasure Isa. 46:10*

God our Creator only does and fulfil what He plans to do and achieve!
Planning prepares the platform for a purposeful existence.
God declared the end from the beginning.
He planned all things to the end before beginning them.
Until you fully plan, do not start.
All things are done according to God's plan and decision (Eph.1:11).
He who fails to prepare prepares to fail.
If you fail to plan, you plan to fail.

To be a person of value demands that you have up-to-date knowledge of your business, the market place and the market need. It is information age, so maximize access to internet information, internet libraries and news media. Up-to-date information and education in your career help you to prepare ahead of any challenge in your field.
The major way to stay relevant is to work harder on yourself than on your job. Attend seminars, whether or not they're company sponsored. Read books. Get a mentor. Add more skills to your current skills set. When you refine your gift into a significant skill, the marketplace will acknowledge and compensate for your effort.
A person of value looks ahead to see the future need of his organisation. Business organizations have multiple and diverse functions. Strive to discover the core purpose that brings in the money and locate a role for yourself there. Identify relevant skills required and possibly scarce and dedicate yourself to acquire those skills. The point is to make yourself so valuable that you become irreplaceable. You need to put yourself in a position that's so vital that the business can't easily discontinue with you. Map out your game plan and follow it through with discipline.
You cannot have a successful week without successful days.
No successful months without successful weeks and no successful year without successful months and weeks.
Success happens when preparation meets opportunity.

### (4) Aim for success
Success does not fall on anyone by accident. It has to be planned.
Plan and prepare to fulfil your destiny by maximizing your potentials.

Apostle Paul confided in us that his success was planned and pursued (1 Cor. 9:26-27). It did not just happen by chance or accident.

God does not require that we be just successful but that we are also faithful in the use of the potentials (talents) that he has endowed us with. The Master in Jesus parable of the talents said to his good stewards, "well done, good and faithful servant (Matt.25:23)!"

It is not enough to be successful or good, you also need to be faithful. True success is becoming a man of purpose. The greatest failure is to be successful in the wrong things. If I employ you to feed my kids and I returned from work to find my kids ignored and unfed while you have cleaned my house and shined everywhere, I will consider you a failure.

You are created for a particular purpose on earth. True success is the result of offering purposeful value to the people you serve through your gift. You carry inside of you a missing part of the puzzle in some people's life. You must develop yourself in such a way that you can reveal that missing part (potential) to solve the people's problems.

If you spend a great time developing yourself, great people will seek you out (Prov.22:29). People come and go in our lives, but we only retain the memory of the few people who make great impacts on our lives.

Be that person that makes an impactful difference in other people's lives. You cannot achieve true success unless you set it up as your goal.

True success consciously begins when you set up the goals you want to achieve in a year and break it down to monthly, weekly and daily goals. Nothing motivates a person like setting up new goals.

Locate and specialize in a field that is blazing the road to the future. A jack of all trade is a master of none.

You should focus strongly on becoming an expert in your field – the area of your purpose and calling. Refuse to be an expert in another man's field while ignoring your own. Charity begins at home.

Then take the progressive step to distinguish yourself.

Do not just be a worker, be "the worker".

Do not just be a specialist, set out to be "the" foremost specialist!

### (5) Live focussed

God is focussed on achieving His purpose only (Isa.46:10).

Valuable people are focussed people. Be focussed!

They focus their actions on adding value to a particular target- be it themselves, their organisation or other people.

They also have a focussed goal that drives all their activities and passion.

No mistake, accident or failure can stop such people on their pursuits. Thomas Edison was a case in view. He experimented with the electric light bulb and failed 10,000 times, but he remained focused on getting a result. He was insulted, mocked but today, we all appreciate his contribution to human civilization.

I am aware that many people have rightly observed that Thomas didn't come up with the first light bulb, but the fact remains that his light bulb was the first that proved practical, and affordable, for home illumination. The team at Edison's "invention factory" in Menlo Park, New Jersey, had been credited for finding a filament that is durable and inexpensive, after testing more than 6,000 possible materials. The lesson learnt here is that quite often; it takes enduring focus to make a valuable contribution to life. We can also learn the fact that sometimes, mistakes are unavoidable in pursuits of exploits. Such mistakes and failures are however an inherent part of success. It is not a waste if you learn from it. It is only a problem if you never learn from them.

Thomas Edison later spoke of his earlier failed tests and attempts, "I have not failed 10,000 times. I have successfully found 10,000 ways that will not work."

Are you devoting your life mostly to that "one thing" you value most? If your life would come to an end today, have you devoted it to the pursuits of your legacy - the one thing, you like to be remembered for? If not, what is wrong with you?

The true purpose is not a matter of employment, but deployment.

A job is an opportunity to get paid while you refine and deploy your gift. Whatever is taking your focus away from the pursuits of your life goal is a diversion. Remember that your time is your life.

It is the way you use your time that you are spending your life. Remember that you cannot recycle time. Focus, now!

**Refine your gift to a niche**

The power of focus is the ability to help you concentrate on your strength. Value is determined by your refined uniqueness.

The way to do this is by making yourself so unique that people won't be able to find any product or services service like yours anywhere else.

The end of preparation is in the perfection of your skill.

That requires continues training and development.

A leader in any field is a lifetime learner. There is room to always upgrade your skill and update yourself with new information.

- Refine your gift till you become an irreplaceable specialist
- Stay focussed on your goal in life (stay away from distractions).
- Find one important thing to master in your profession every week
- Improve yourself socially, mentally, physically etc.
- Eliminate time wasters and diversions and guard your time
- Plan at least one full day to rest weekly to recover your strength and refresh your mind. It helps you to focus the more.

**(6) Serve your gift in the best way possible**
The more values you put in life, the more valuable you become.
Most people have great visions. What's lacking is pursuits.
Make yourself valuable to your organisation.
The more you help people to solve their problems, the more valuable you become. You will succeed when you assist others in achieving their mission and fulfil their needs. Different people will come from everywhere to your unique gift when you make yourself valuable.
A shining candle is a burning candle. To shine and give light to others, a candle has to diminish through his sacrifice.
The same should be true with your work.
Always keep in mind the ultimate goal you're working towards and the benefits that come with it. That offers strength for endurance.

---

**To be unique, you need to be yourself.**
**Everybody is meant to be "the" Principal Actor of his life.**
**To be authentic,**
you need to genuinely stick to your original purpose.
**To be valuable, you need to be the best of yourself.**
**To remain relevant,**
you need to continue to improve yourself.

### Give your best!
- Find the best strategy to serve your gifts.
- Volunteer and participate in your company programs.
- Find ways to make your accomplishments visible to your leaders.
- Always be willing to accept new challenges and assignments.

### (7) Live on purpose
Most frustrated people do not lack vision or success but only miss fulfilment because they are mostly not living on purpose.

They are mostly hard-working people seeking success, but somehow they always seem to miss their target or hit the wrong mark. They are mostly focussed on success more than purpose. The problem with success is that the excitement from it is often ephemeral. Even when people compete successfully, if they do not see any connection between that success and their life purpose, it might lead to frustration and sadness.

I read a story about The Beatles leader, John Lennon who at the peak of his career considered himself a great failure. He simply felt empty inside though he was a world-acclaimed superstar. We have many simple, unknown people who are quite satisfied with their lives.

The point I am making here is that life usually feels pleasant and fulfilling when your success matches your purpose and value system.

### Live consciously

*Teach us to number our days, which we may gain a heart of wisdom. Psalm 90:12*

Mastering your time on earth adds wisdom to your conduct.
Living purposely is about living wisely with time.
Every purpose has a limited time to achieve. So is also your life.
You do not have forever to live. Every second brings you closer to the end of your existence. You must achieve your purpose within your given time. You should therefore master the way you use time.

### a) Master the art of Time Management
Time remains the most valuable commodity in life. Valuable people make the most of the time by acquiring skill and wisdom.
You need to protect your time from time wasters.

You also need to master the art of buying other people's time to save yours. Wisdom is in spending your time on the things you bear maximum return and buying other people's time on things you are not so good in. Rich people always buy and maximize other people's resources especially their time.

b)  **Master the art of time Investment**
The major secret behind lives of great believers is their time investment with God (Matt 6:33). They invested much of their temporal time in creating eternal relationship and values.
It is only the time you invest in the presence of God or in the things of God that is eternal. More than that, it is your time investment in God that guarantees you blessed and long life on earth. Nothing else does. Insurance can insure your life but cannot protect or extend it. God can! When you invest time in God's service, He promises to give you long life (Exodus 23: 25-27.) Even if your life expired and you need more, only God can add more years to your life. He added fifteen more years to the life of Hezekiah (2 Kings 20:1-7).

**(8)  Maintain a professional network**
Two significant things will make a difference between who you are today and where you will be in ten years, the books you read and the people you network with. No matter what might be changing in your career or environment, all you need to do is take responsibility for change.
It will always be helpful to have around you progressive people that can help you stay on course. The network helps you to synergize.
The network may come in different forms.

a)  **Mentorship**
Isaac Newton stated the immediate benefit of mentorship when he said, "If I see farther it is because I stand on shoulders of giants."
Mentorship is about leveraging other people's ability and capacity. Whoever walks with the wise becomes wise (Prov. 13:20a).
In the Bible, Abraham mentored Lot. Eli mentored Samuel. Naomi mentored Ruth, Moses mentored Joshua, Deborah mentored Barak, Elijah mentored Elisha and Mordecai mentored Queen Esther. Elizabeth mentored Mary (the mother of Jesus Christ), and Jesus Christ Himself mentored His 12 disciples.

After the days of Jesus Christ, Barnabas briefly mentored Paul and Apostle Paul himself went on to mentor Timothy.

Mentorship is a Christian lifestyle and it is meant to become at home with parents mentoring (training) their children (Prov.22:6).

Advantages of mentorship include:
- Training ground for professional skill development
- Positive edge in solving problems and new challenges
- Hand on of first-hand experience, skills and supports
- Enjoy different perspective at seeing problems and situations
- Offer fresh insights
- Expand network and can connect to new contacts
- Offer a chance for mutual improvements and benefits

**b) Counselling**

Counselling is another way of profiting from other people's experience. Counselling refers to the opinion or advice given by others in directing our judgment or conducts. The difference between a successful business and non-successful business is in the information they have access to. Jethro, the father-in-law of Moses, counselled him on how to reduce his burden of leadership and delegate responsibilities for minor cases to his other leaders. This helped to relieve Moses of the great burden that could have caused him a burnout.

Parts of the benefits of counselling include:
- Sort out your thoughts and bring clarity to issues
- Help to set and achieve your goals
- Offer strategies to develop your full potential
- Offer brainstorming, the synergy of intelligence and experience
- Help to develop a realistic plan of action to move forward
- Give you a greater degree of self-awareness and sense of direction
- Improve self-esteem and confidence

## Set up a mastermind group

No mind is complete by itself. One way of enjoying network at its highest level is to form a team of a mastermind to work together. Everyone needs association with other people to grow and expand. The idea behind creating a mastermind group is to put like-minded great minds together to create something more powerful than the sum of those individual minds.

Mastermind is the power of plugging into each other, then watching the collective units create many more solutions than they ever could on their own. Most wealthy people belong to a Mastermind group from whom they received support, encouragement and advice. Jesus' had his disciples. Jacob had his mother, and together they outsmarted Esau and won the heart of Isaac. The world's most successful and most famous people always surround themselves with mastermind network made up of strategic people who have made it to the top of their careers.

The legendary King Arthur (British leader in the late 5$^{th}$ century) set up Knights of the Round Table made up of 25 best knights in his kingdom. Walt Disney (a pioneer of the American animation industry) had his 9 Old men made up of 9 talented animators who were behind Walt Disney most iconic works. Benjamin Franklin (one of the founding fathers of the United States) formed the "Leather Apron Club" also known as "the Junto" made up of 12 members whose focus is to seek improvements among themselves. And of course, Thomas Edison had his club, "The vagabonds" consisting of Henry Ford, John Burroughs and Harvey Firestones. They regularly come to discuss their business ventures.

You will also need to set up your mastermind to stay stronger and more competitive in your area of practice.

Some of the advantages of mastermind include:

- Engaging in critical strategic thinking with like-minded people
- Using people with experience in different fields to test your ideas
- Rich ability to share diverse ideas, different scenarios and strategies
- Enjoying the synergy of ideas from great minds
- Enjoying a learning opportunity with every new interaction
- Removing noise is essential for success
- Understand things that could have taken a longer time
- Enjoying life experience and insights of other visionaries

Good human relationship offers great reward always.
It however requires mutual understanding and commitment to build.
Learn to revere, respect and honour people around you.
It grants you access to what they carry.
Learn to relate and co-operate with other people around you. It grants you synergy that can explosively increase your potentials.
Maximize the wealth in other people and use the acquired skill, insights and other advantages to bless humanity.

### (9) Live with a legacy mind-set

To make the best of your potentials, you need to be legacy-minded. Our greatest example was the Lord Jesus Christ while he was on earth. He endured the cross focussing on the joy set before Him (Heb.12:2). You need to be prepared to endure all the pains and opposition you will encounter on your way to the great future set ahead of you.

Nothing great can be built in one day. Every great thing requires following a due process. You need to resolve never to quit regardless of any shame and mockery you may meet amid your pursuits.

To do that, you must have a big picture of what you are exchanging your life for so that as you take one step at a time, you do not lose motivation or get your attention diverted.

How often, do you see people who started well not ending well!

The end of a thing is better than the beginning. It is a shame to miss it! Finishers are winners. Finishing is more important than starting.

Winners don't quit and quitters don't win. Some are distracted by the rat race of life and get lost in the competition. They forget that in the race of life, you have only yourself to compete against.

That is because none of us is running the same race.

Everyone is uniquely endowed for a unique race!

Some end up losing focus to greed, avariciousness and cheap life.

The secret of winning is to stay focused on your purpose of existence.

Think of your legacy from the onset.

There are so many blessings for living with a legacy mind-set.

### a) Employment

Only those who deploy themselves can employ others.

Employment is a product of deployment.

Deployment is the only cure for unemployment.

Until your potential is deployed, it cannot employ you or any other person. Only a man who is yet to deploy self fears unemployment.

The first product of a perfect deployment of potentials is self-employment. A well deployed potential first employs its carrier.

The continuous deployment of potential, in forms of products and services, soon become a lasting source of employment for other people.

### b) Joy and satisfaction.

More than salary, there is joy in deploying your potential. Every service and product is a deployment of someone's potential. It is someone giving birth to ideas and solutions hidden inside her or him as potentials. There is a sense of fulfilment every time you complete a project or work.

**c) Valuable existence**
Life is only meaningful when it serves the purpose it is created for.
You are not given a driven licence, salary or a college degree because you are old; you are only rewarded with such because you qualify.
It is also the same with your life. You will be compensated for achieving the purpose of your life is designed for.
The number of years does not count, only the impact counts.
The legacy of a good deployment of potential is in the value it continues to add to other people. A well deployed potential leaves a good legacy of value-added service and products.
We are meant to make the world a better place than we met it. Purposeful people believe they owe a debt to their society and are committed to paying it. The value of life is in investing it in creating better lives for both ourselves and the other people around us.

## Keep result in sight

- No man is born to live unto himself alone. A life lived for God leaves a lasting legacy of light. Think legacy as you deploy yourself.
- We are created to produce seeds after our type. We are to pass on our legacy to others by sowing our lives as seeds into their lives. Whatever you do should be done with the heart to benefit someone.
- The only thing you take with you out of this life is the legacy you leave behind. That is what it means to have a fruitful life that is multiplied in the lives of others.
- Mostly to have a good legacy, you need to selfless invest into others. You have to sacrifice your life in serving others.

## Balancing Your Potential, Destiny and Purpose

Since God will judge every man according to the purpose He sends each to serve on earth and not necessarily according to what a man chooses to do; the greatest achievement is to serve God's purpose for your life.
It is those who stay faithful to their purposes that are the true success!

- Enjoying a purposeful existence begins with effective potential development. Potential is the container carrying your future. It is the carrier of the entire capacity to fulfil your destiny and purpose.

- The fulfilment of your destiny is attached to your potentials. A successful destiny is attained through the discovery, development and the deployment of your potentials.
- To enjoy life fulfilment, you need to use your destiny to fulfil God's purpose for your life. Success is not enough if it does not fulfil. Same way, successful destiny is not enough if it does not fulfil the purpose of life.

Self-fulfilment is the destination of self-discovery, self-development and self-deployment. The essence of discovering your gifts and talents is to provoke you to develop it to the best of your ability and deploy it to add great values to other people through the services and products your life purpose assigns to you to serve your nation and generation.

While success is a good thing, it does not mean the same as fulfilment. Many people's source of tragedy in life is being successful in the wrong things. How often that the so-called successful people can go through life, disappointed, wounded and frustrated. That is the logical conclusion to running another man's race instead of focussing on running your God-given race. No matter how fast or strong you are in running another man's race, you will feel frustrated at the end.

Worse still, you may still face disgrace at the end of the race when you are denied any recognition or trophy for running the wrong race.

May you never waste your life running the wrong race.

May selfish ambition and greed never force you to end up in the rat race of life. May you be focussed enough to run your race with all your ability and might to the very end. That is the only way to enjoy fulfilment in this life and in the one to come.

The goal of successfully developing your potential is to fulfil your destiny. And the purpose of your destiny is to fulfil God's purpose. There is a purpose for your life and it is when you use your destiny to fulfil that purpose that you can enjoy fulfilment.

Only those who can pursue their potential development to the joyful end of using it to enrich their personal life and achieve the purpose of God can experience the satisfaction of self-fulfilment.

That is a true success every believer should aspire to achieve.

The only time a product or a person enjoys fulfilment is when it fulfils the purpose it is designed to serve. It is my prayer that you fulfil your potential and enjoy a fulfilled life. Amen.

## PRINCIPLES FOR BECOMING A PERSON OF VALUE

1) The essence of discovering, developing and deploying your potential is to become a person of value.

2) A person of value is a principled person guided by moral values.

3) A value system is a set of ideas that guide your behaviour.

4) The greatest discovery in life is self-discovery.

5) It's your uniqueness that ultimately makes you valuable.

6) To remain a person of value demands that you continuously go through a process of developing yourself to serve your gift in the best way.

7) The more values you put in life, the more valuable you become.

8) Most frustrated people do not lack vision or success but only miss fulfilment because they are mostly not living on purpose.

9) To make the best of your potentials, you need to be legacy-minded.

10) Only those who deploy themselves can employ others.

11) Life is only meaningful when it serves the purpose it is created for.

12) Since every man will be judged by God according to the purpose he is sent to serve on earth and not necessarily what he chooses to do, the greatest achievement is to serve God's purpose for your life.

## CHAPTER 14: BLESSED BY CHOICE

*For by grace you have been saved through faith. And this is not your own doing; it is the gift of God. Ephesians 2:8*

God's grace is simply unmerited favour of God towards us. The saving grace of God to man is a gift - an outpouring of His faithfulness. No man can ever earn this favour by labour. Nobody can claim to be alive without benefiting from God's grace. Another word for God's grace is God's "unconditional love." God loves us because God is love not because of what we are. Another word for God's grace is God's undeserved blessing. Every blessing of God upon mankind is by grace! They are never earned but freely given as His token of love. Bible teaches some important truths about God's blessing.

a) God's blessings are expressions of God's grace
God's blessing is a gift of grace. As could be seen in the encounter of Mary, the mother of Jesus Christ with God, it is a product of favour (Luke 1: 28-30). No matter how righteous or pious Mary could have been, no woman deserves to be the mother of Jesus Christ except by God by grace. It is Out of the fullness of His grace He has blessed us all, giving us one blessing after another (John 1:16). That you are born into this world is by grace. You or your parents do not earn it. It is a blessing of the Lord. That is why the Bible says, "Children are a gift from the LORD (Psalm 127:3)." That you wake up in the morning is not earned. It is a blessing. That you are healthy is a blessing. Nobody can claim to have earned his health. All these blessings are priceless products of God's grace.

b) God's blessings are associated with God's presence
Where God's presence dwells is where His blessings flow. In His presence is the fullness of joy. If you can make your environment God friendly enough to attract His presence, you will soon be flowing in His blessings. The angel that ministered to Mary associated her favour with the presence of God. The Lord is with you (Luke 1:28)!

c) God's systems run by the grace
The Angel of the Lord assured Mary that her body system would produce a Saviour (Luke 1:31). God's grace easily runs through his system.

Any system created by God is sustained by Him. His power runs through His systems to deliver. Our body system operates on priceless but free air throughout our lifetime. That is a miracle. Every blessing of God springs out of God's being as a free grace.

d)   God's gifts and endowments are by grace
God's gifts, talents and mercies are all expressions of His love.
In the story of the talents, none of the stewards deserves or qualifies for any particular amount of talents. It was the master's decision.
Jesus rode only on one donkey to Jerusalem in his last days. What a great donkey, but the success story has God as the sole Author. The donkey did not choose itself or do anything special to qualify than other donkeys. Bible also recorded the only donkey that ever spoke in the history of this world (Numbers 22: 21-33). What a wonderful donkey. But its greatness has nothing to do with its unique qualification or skill. It is rather a product of being in the right place at the right time to be used by God. How often you see ignorant carriers of God's grace boasting of their accomplishments and exploits without giving the glory to the Giver of all gifts and talents. Such is not responding wisely to the grace of God.

## Responding to God's grace

*But by the grace of God I am what I am: and his grace which was bestowed upon me was not in vain; but I laboured more abundantly than they all: yet not I, but the grace of God which was with me. 1 Cor. 15:10*

Never take the grace of God in vain!
In the Kingdom of God, the blessing is a gift - a product of God's kindness. Before the first men know what life is all about, God blessed them. Blessing is a proof of His faithfulness.
How we respond to His blessing proofs our faithfulness.
The grace of God is not meant to be a bed of rose where you lay and relax for the rest of your life neither is it meant to be a Swing that rocks you back and forth in the same spot in euphoria; rather it is meant to be an empowering force that drives you forward in life to become a valuable person in the pursuits of God's purpose for your life.
The lifestyle of good people is like sunlight at dawn that keeps getting brighter until broad daylight. (Prov.4:18- C.E.V). The moving force behind such progressive life is the grace of God. Grace is not given to us in vain. There is a right and wrong way to respond to God's grace.

> In the Kingdom of God, the blessing is a gift - a product of God's kindness. Before the first men know what life is all about, God blessed them.
> **Blessing is a proof of His faithfulness.**
> How we respond to His blessing proofs our faithfulness.

## The right response to God's grace

God's grace and love are generously given to us by God and can never be earned by a man. In the Kingdom of God, you do not earn blessing by your sheer work (Eph.2:8-9). Blessing is a gift of the King to all His citizens (sons). You receive a blessing because of God's goodness and faithfulness.

The Christian faith calls believers to embark on the path of spiritual maturity rather than retardation. After receiving salvation, you are instructed to "keep yourselves in the love of God, looking for the mercy of our Lord Jesus Christ unto eternal life." (Jude 21).

### 1) Appreciation

The first response to grace is to show gratitude for the restoration back to fellowship with God. To be disconnected from God is to live in death. For giving us life, we need to be grateful.

Nobody is qualified to be alive; it is by grace you are here. And when the first man Adam lost the right to be in the presence of God forever through sin and disobedience Jesus Christ by His obedience to God fulfilled the righteous requirements of the law for us even when it cost His life. We owe God gratitude for granting us life on earth as well as eternal life after existence on earth.

The foremost response of gratitude is to know God and share a relationship of love and intimacy with Him. You are not born again to slave for God; rather, you are born again as a son of God to enjoy a fresh relationship with your Heavenly Father (John 17:3).

You were primarily saved to enjoy an intimate relationship with God.

### 2) Service to God (work of faith)

The joy of God bubbling inside of us is meant to spill out into service to Him (1 Cor.15:58). This natural response to serve God is not the same as carrying the burden of dead religious works. God relates with us based on His mercy and not on that of our works. Our urge to serve God flows from our appreciation and love for Him.

Our work of faith is a work of appreciation in response to what God has done for us. When God created humanity in His image, He mandated man out of overflowing love to rule the earth in His stead.

Service is never meant to be a legalistic demand from a narcissistic God; rather it is meant to be a creative way of exploring and exposing the divine potentials that God deposited inside His precious creature.

Work is given to man as a tool for creativity by which man can share in the divine nature. God and Jesus worked (John 5:17)!

True work of faith is a grateful response to God's greatness.

Service is a wise response to the grace of God. It commits God to man! It is a major key to walking in divine blessing. God's faithful promise remains to bless whoever serves Him (Exodus 23:25).

### 3) Service to mankind (work of love)

God expects the overflowing abundance we receive to flow into the lives of other people through our service.

The Bible says we are created in Christ Jesus to do good works. In the same way, we appreciate Jesus Christ for sacrificing His life to save us all do we continue to appreciate the self-sacrifice and selfless service of other people. Jesus taught his disciples that whosoever wants to be great shall be a servant of all (Matt.20:26, 28). Every believer walking in the footsteps of Jesus Christ needs to learn to serve others in a church community (Heb.10:25, Gal. 6:10). The church allows us to get involved in the work and passion of Jesus Christ.

Even though no church is perfect, like no person is perfect, the church is nonetheless purposefully created by God to help us stay committed to the process of perfection in our earthly journey with Jesus Christ.

In Church we are given the opportunity to grow in faith and the fruits of the spirit. The church gives us opportunities to worship God together, find out His purpose for our lives, support each other, complement each other in saving lost souls and acquire fruits of the spirit as we daily perfect our characters etcetera.

Since eternity is about living with God forever, we have the Church as a practice ground to learn how to live and share our experiences since we are going to co-exist in God's presence forever.

Our service however is not meant to end in Church.

We are called to serve the whole world. Since we are created in the image and likeness of God, we are to become a channel through which God's grace can continue to flow into the lives of others. We are God's handiwork, created in Christ Jesus to do good works, which God prepared in advance for us to do (Eph.2:10). We do good work for grace makes us extension of God's goodness. We participate in the work of God in winning lost souls as a "co-laborers."

## Call to serve in grace

We are called to follow the example of Jesus Christ in our work of grace. None of us deserves God's mercy and grace, yet Jesus Christ makes it available to everyone in the whole world. When people therefore fall beside us, God expects us to lift them following Jesus standard, "for while we were still sinners, Christ died for us (Romans 5:8)".
Jesus came to the world so that no man may perish but that we may all have everlasting life (John3:16). We are not called to judge others! Jesus warned us to judge not so we may not be judged (Matt.7:1-3).
We are to selflessly lead people into repentance and restoration and not into judgement. We are to consciously extend God's grace to our families, friends, neighbours, colleagues, and other people that might come in contact with us.

## The wrong response to God's grace

> *For if we sin wilfully after that we have received the knowledge of the truth, there remaineth no more sacrifice for sins, 27 But a certain fearful looking for of judgment and fiery indignation, which shall devour the adversaries. Hebrews 10:26-27*

While this dispensation of Grace lasts, we will continue to know God as the God of Grace. His grace will continue to be sufficient to recover from any loss we might suffer. But when this grace dispensation or our life expires, we are not going to know Him any more as God of grace. He will return as the Judge to whom all must give stewardship account of their use of potentials. Misusing God's grace is wrong.
There are major ways we could misuse or abuse God's grace.

a) Living in sin

*Teaching us that, denying ungodliness and worldly lusts, we should live soberly, righteously, and godly, in this present world. Titus 2:12*

Romans 6:1-2 says, "What shall we say then? Are we to continue in sin that grace may abound? To continue to live in sin under the false principle of eternal salvation- once save always save- or any other excuse is an abuse of grace. As clearly explained in the book of Hebrews, "For if we go on sinning deliberately after receiving the knowledge of the truth, there no longer remains a sacrifice for sins, but a fearful expectation of judgment, and a fury of fire that will consume the adversaries (Heb.10:26-27)." The grace of God trains us "to renounce ungodliness and worldly passions and to live self-controlled, upright, and godly lives in the present age.

A true believer can temporarily fall in to sin, but he will repent and return to God. The apostates - those taking God's grace in vain will continue to sin, deliberately, willingly and with abandon. Jesus described those apostates in His parables of the sower as the people who "receive with joy" the things of the Lord, but who are drawn away by the cares of the world and the difficulties they encounter because of Christ (Matthew 13:20-21). The true apostates are those believers who know the way of God, count themselves as among the faithful, and continue to sin wilfully without repentance. Apostates do not sin because of ignorance or momentary temptations but live in sin wilfully. Such apostate is beyond salvation because he has rejected Jesus sacrifice for sins. Once Jesus sacrifice for sin and offer of salvation is rejected, the only thing a man is left with is sin and the consequence of it which is eternal death.

b) Wasting potentials

*And we know that all things work together for good to them that love God, to them who are the called according to his purpose. Rom.8:28*

No matter the mistakes and the failures of the past, so long we choose to walk according to His purpose; all things will work together for our good. That is how loving and faithful God is to us. We all still have time, to obey the instruction of the Master (God), "'Put this money (potentials) to work,' he said, 'until I come back (Luke 19:13b)"

God equipped us for success. He is interested in our purposeful end.
We are to redeem the time for the days are evil.
We are to make hay while the sun shines (Prov.10:5).

## Choosing the blessing

*Blessed is the man who does not walk in the counsel of the wicked or stand in the way of sinners or sit in the seat of mockers. 2 But his delight is in the law of the LORD, and on his law he meditates day and night. 3 He is like a tree planted by streams of water, which yields its fruit in season and whose leaf does not wither. Whatever he does prospers. Psalm 1:1-3*

While blessing is a gift, it is a gift that is easily attracted to a particular lifestyle of those who have chosen to the path of blessing.
Blessing means God's supernatural empowerment to make you accomplish what you are created to do. And God blessed them, and God said unto them, Be fruitful, and multiply, and replenish the earth, and subdue it: and have dominion over the fish of the sea, and over the fowl of the air, and over every living thing that moves upon the earth (Gen. 1:28).
God's blessing is therefore the solution to all forms of curses.
Curses are supernatural disempowerment to make you not achieve what you are created to achieve).
If you understand that definition of blessing, you will never suffer a wasted night worrying about curses from the devil and his evil forces.
Only God occupies the department of blessing and He has blessed us.
All we can do is to activate or deactivate that blessing through our actions and inactions and the consequences they bring upon our lives.
In essence, you are already blessed by the Most High God.
If you continue to walk in blessing or not is your choice.

### 1) God's original intent for everyman is to walk in blessing
The blessing of the Lord came before the mandate of God!
Even before He spoke the first word to man, God blessed them!
In the story of the talents told by Jesus Christ (Matt.25:14), the Master in the story (representing God) gave the servants (representing man) the talents (blessings, gifts, grace etc.) even before they ever did anything.
Blessing remains God's original plan for all His creatures.
The blessing of the Lord makes rich and he adds no sorrow unto it.

God's original intent for His creature is for him to walk in prosperity in every area of life - your health, wealth, joyful relationships, fulfilment etc. Sin, sickness and curses are the consequence of human disobedience and fall. Now that Jesus Christ has paid for human disobedience and restored us to God, no man needs to suffer the burden of disobedience anymore. Any man who chooses to obey God can walk in blessing.

## 2) Nobody- not even devil- can curse whom God has blessed

Like King Balaak (in the Bible) found out when he called on prophet Balaam to curse God's blessed people, "God is not a man, that He should lie, or a son of man, that He should change His mind!"

Once God has blessed you, you remain blessed (Num. 23:18-30, 24:1-13). God will never go back on His promises.

He is forever faithful to bring to pass all His promises.

You should rather focus your attention on walking consciously in the blessing of God by doing what God has blessed or promised to bless.

Stop worrying about the curse from your enemies.

The curse causeless shall not come (Prov.26:2).

Any curse you do not cause or deserve shall not harm you just like a bird flying over your head cannot harm you.

Such undeserved curses will only return to torment the sender!

Rather than being troubled about curses, follow Jesus Christ advice and bless your enemies. So long God is with you, no enemy can touch you. The Psalmist says, "You prepare a table before me in the presence of my enemies; you anoint my head with oil; my cup runs over. 6 Surely goodness and mercy shall follow me All the days of my life; And I will dwell in the house of the Lord Forever (Psalm 25:5-6)".

The blessing of the Lord supersedes all.

No one can curse whom the Lord has blessed.

Despite the devil and your enemy, you can enjoy running over blessing. Goodness and mercy will follow you all the days of your life so long you chose to dwell in the house of the Lord forever more.

It is fear born out of ignorance that makes people run Hester Kester worrying from being troubled by the enemy (devil) and his spiritual and human messengers. If God is for you, no one can be against you!

You should instead be investing your time running after God than running away from the devil. Devil will never come near you if he knows you are in the presence of God. In His presence is the fullness of joy!

No curse or evil can stand with you in God's presence.

### 3) The blessing of the Lord is His supernatural power to make!

*The blessing of the LORD, it maketh rich, and he addeth no sorrow with it.*
*Proverbs 10:22*

Blessing is the divine empowerment to make His creature become what it is created to be. And the proof of God's blessing is that it brings no sorrow. In the presence of the Lord is only fullness of joy.
The blessing of the Lord is a proof of God's faithfulness to mankind.
The first thing God did to His first creatures was to bless them.
It can then be rightly stated that God wants His creatures to walk in blessing. If we do is a choice we have to make by ourselves.
Sometimes we think of a blessing as something earned or deserved.
In reality, it is always linked with favour.
God's favour is always being attracted to good labours.
God blesses no evil.

### 4) Every time God blesses, it is to fulfil His promise

God is forever faithful. He will fulfil all His promises.
Every time God blesses, it is to authenticate His personality and integrity and to confirm His promises. That is why walking in obedience to God's promises easily attract His blessing to people.
God is faithful to His words (Psalm 138:2; Isaiah 55:11).
God connected the pregnancy of Mary to His earlier promise to save humanity (Matthew 1:20-23).
God will always fulfil His promises and bless His purpose.
Anytime a person aligns self to the presence, purpose or promise of God, he connects to God's power.
To walk in God's promise and purpose is to walk in blessing by choice.

### 5) The level, extent and tenure of God's blessing a man can access are consequent on every man's obedience

The level and extent of God's blessing that you will enjoy in this life and eternity will be a reward of your reaction to God's instruction.
It is consequent on your faithful conduct to the Lord of the Kingdom.
Though God can do exceeding and abundantly and above human expectation and desire, it is however at the end, unto every one according to his or her level of faithfulness. Though the thought of giving birth to the world's saviour understandably was too big for Mary, yet she accepted Angel's explanation that the Holy Spirit would bring the

promise to past. The same stands for us today. By the Power of the Holy Spirit, every promise of the Lord will surely come to past.

### 6)  Every time God blesses, it is meant to bless others
God promised to bless Abram so that he can be a blessing to others (Gen.12:2). Forty years after Moses had been living in obscurity as a refugee outside the home; his joy of hearing from God was short lived when he heard that God has returned to him in the response of the cries of the children of Israel. The reason for the blessed meeting is for other people to be blessed through Moses (Exodus 3:7-10).

The good news to Mary is meant to be good news to the whole world – even to the several generations to come after her (Luke 2:10).

### 7)  God's ultimate blessing is for you to share eternity with Him
The purpose of Jesus Christ for coming to the world is not to judge the world but to make sure that no man perishes. God mainly gave Jesus Christ to the world that whoever believes in him should not perish but have eternal life (John 3:16). God is interested in you making eternity. The evil one came to the world to distort that plan by causing disobedience, diversion and destruction but the Lord Jesus Christ came to repair so that we can have access to abundant life.

Eternity is the inbuilt potential of all spiritual beings created in the image and likeness of God. That was what died in Adam and Eve when they fell into sin in the Garden of Eden. That was what Jesus Christ restored to mankind when He gave His life on the cross and resurrected.

That is what you should prioritize in your lifetime. Of what profit shall life be for a man who gains everything in the world and lose his soul? Vanity, everything without the safety of your soul is vanity.

Everything on earth is temporary. You will leave everything behind once. Only the time and the thing you invest in the Lord will remain eternally in your account forever. Only your relationship and encounters with God will remain eternal. Only the work and souls you save will remain with you forever. Only your spiritual values will remain eternal.

Salvation is more than being restored to God. It is about remaining solidly rooted in Him for where you are grounded, is where you end up. Where you put your heart, hope, love, treasure while alive is where you will end up at the end of life.  That is why a believer's walk with God is meant to be a relationship and not a religion.

There is nothing greater than sharing eternity with the Lord.

## Prioritize your relationship with your Maker!

If you also treasure enjoying your eternity with the Lord, then prioritize your relationship with Him more than any other person or thing.
He alone has the key to the prosperity of your body, soul and spirit.
Your parents can train you up in life
Your friends can help and support your life
Your employer can bankroll your life
A doctor can medically support your life
A teacher can improve your knowledge.
An insurance agent can insure your life
A law enforcement agent can protect your life
A lawyer can defend your life
A pastor can guide your life
But only God can give you a long life on earth and everlasting life in eternity. It is only a personal relationship with God that guarantees your blessing on earth and thereafter. Seek the Lord when He can be found! What shall it profit a man who gains the whole world and loses his soul in eternity? The greatest blessing is to enjoy the eternity with the Lord in addition to all the victories God has provided for us on earth.
Enjoying eternity with the Lord is an eternal blessing with no end.

## Keep walking in blessing

*What, then, shall we say in response to these things? If God is for us, who can be against us? Romans 8:31 (NIV)*

And if God is for you, who can be against you?
To live a blessed life by choice is to choose to walk in the blessing!
The cheapest way to walk in blessing is to continue to do what God has blessed or promised to bless.

### a) Desire passionately to be useful for God's purpose

Your genuine desire to serve God's purpose qualifies you for His use. Becoming a candidate for God's blessing is not an accident. How much of a blessing that you receive is based upon your deep desire?
The delight (of this man blessed) is in the law of the LORD, and on his law, he meditates day and night (Psalm 1:2).
God mostly do not use the qualified so they will not boast of their abilities. God mostly uses the willing and qualifies them with whatever potential they need to perform the duties of their office. It was after God sent

Samuel to anoint King Saul and King David that the spirit of God enters them. That was where they secured wisdom to lead God's people, not from their poor shepherd background.

*As Saul turned to leave Samuel, God changed Saul's heart, and all the signs came to pass that day. 10When Saul and his servant arrived at Gibeah,c a group of prophets met him. Then the Spirit of God rushed upon him, and he prophesied along with them. 1 Sam.10:9-10*

*So Samuel took the horn of oil and anointed him in the presence of his brothers, and from that day on the Spirit of the LORD came powerfully upon David. Samuel then went to Ramah. 1 Sam.16:13*

Once God sees a genuine desire to serve His purpose in a person or a thing, he uses them! It does not matter your past mistakes or failure.
It does not bother God how people see you; God still sees His potential in you. The only thing that disqualifies a man from being used by God is his desire not to be used. And God will not force you!
But so long your heart willingly opens up to serve God, He will use you. He created you for a purpose on earth. No matter how people see you, you still carry the potentials to achieve that purpose.
God sees differently from the way man sees.
I read something so inspiring recently about the man Joseph in the Bible.
Jacob, his father, saw in him, a bright son.
The ten brothers saw a troublesome dreamer.
Potiphar saw a faithful slave.
Potiphar's wife saw a secret lover.
The prison warden saw in Joseph, a trustworthy prisoner.
Other prisoners saw a close confidant.
Pharaoh saw a competent administrator.
God saw a faithful steward that can lead others out of bondage. Yes, Joseph was in prison but with God took him from there to the Palace!
God is not bothered by your bad past.
He used Moses, a murderer and Apostle Paul (former Saul), a persecutor of His chosen people.
God does not discriminate with age. He called Abram at the age of 75.
He is not bothered by experience; He chose a young David as king.
He is not bothered by your gender; He used Esther to save the Jews.

His hands are not bound by your religion. He used King Cyrus a non-believer with a genuine heart for the things of God.
God is not even bothered about the difference in creation. He used a donkey to talk to Balaam. All that moves God is your willingness to serve His purpose with the potentials he has put inside you.

### b) Walk in obedience
To receive God's blessings, there must be obedience to God.
A blessed man is the one who chooses not to walk the path of sinners and mockers. A blessed person is the one who has chosen to walk the path of truth and obedience. He is a person committed to seeking the presence of God as he meditates day and night. Such a person knows that the Lord is only attracted to the way of a righteous person.
The way of the wicked God causes to perish (Psalm 1:6).
Obedience simply activates God's blessing.
Open your Bible today and study everywhere that started with, "Blessed are…" Fill in your name and keep fulfilling the term of the covenant. Begin with Deuteronomy 28:1-14, and Matthew 5:3-16.

### c) Be diligent in the pursuits of God's purpose
That you are kept alive is God's proof of faithfulness. Your willingness to use your potentials in the purpose of God is proof of your faithfulness. It is your response to Him in the form of your service and gratitude that demonstrates your faithfulness back to God.
Remember it is expected that a steward is found faithful (1 Cor.4:2).
In the story of the talents, Jesus Christ narrated, the two faithful servants doubled their blessings while the lazy one lost even his original blessing (Matt.25:19-30). Stop blaming God, man and your environment for your situation. Focus inside and put a demand on your talent.
Your talent has an answer to every situation of life.
God has faithfully deposited sufficient talents (potentials) to help you scale through the challenges of life.
God can do immeasurably more than all we ask or imagine, according to His power (potentials) that is at work within us!
Your solution is not in those people you are looking at rather it is in the potential God already deposited inside of you (Eph. 3:20)!

**d) Maximize your opportunities by making the best use of them.**
The best God can give a man is an opportunity. Opportunity is the greatest gift you will ever have to become anything in this life.
It is an opportunity that we convert to health, wealth fame and other substance of life. Our works are meant to display our appreciation of God's kindness and faithfulness to us. You receive God's blessing to empower you to fulfil the purpose God predestined you for (Eph.2.10). The servant who had received the five talents went and put them to work and gained five more. 17 Likewise, the one with the two talents gained two more. 18 But the servant who had received the one talent went off, dug a hole in the ground, and hid his master's money (Matt.25:16-18). Thinking he was sabotaging the Master, the servant with "entitlement mentality" refused to appreciate the privilege given to him to serve. While other servants were busy raising the bars of their blessing, he closed the lid upon his blessing and buried it.
The only way to prove your worthiness is to increase your blessing not to sabotage, hide or waste it. To destroy any chance given you anywhere is to sabotage your destiny.

---

**To live a blessed life by choice is to choose to walk in the blessing!
The cheapest way to walk in blessing is to continue to do what God has blessed or promised to bless.**

**PRINCIPLES OF BLESSING**

1) The blessing of the Lord is His supernatural power to make!

2) Becoming a candidate for God's blessing is not an accident.

3) The blessing of the Lord is a product of favour.

4) Divine favour is connected with the presence of God

5) Every time God blesses, it is to fulfil His promise and to authenticate His truth.

6) The right response to God's blessing is joy and commitment to serve

7) Every time God blesses, it is meant to be a means of blessing others.

8) God's blessing is an expression of His faithfulness.

9) The blessing of the Lord came before the mandate of God!

10) If you continue to walk in blessing or not is your choice

11) The level, extent and tenure of God's blessing a man can access are consequent on every man's obedience and disobedience.

12) God's ultimate blessing is for you to share eternity with Him.

## CONCLUSION: Grace for the race

*For by grace are ye saved through faith; and that not of yourselves: it is the gift of God: 9 Not of works, lest any man should boast. 10 For we are his workmanship, created in Christ Jesus unto good works, which God hath before ordained that we should walk in them. Ephesians 2:8-10*

Grace is the kingdom's joker for prevailing in the race of life. No matter what you are going through, God's grace is ever sufficient. Grace supersedes work.
One time favour is worth more than a lifetime of labour!
God's grace released the people of Israel from four hundred and thirty years bondage just in one day. Grace makes the difference.
It was the grace of God upon the life of Joseph that turned him from prisoner to a minister of state serving in the King's palace.
Grace makes great. The grace of God at work in a man's life makes the journey of life great.
God's grace can turn captives to captors and turns zeros to heroes.
It can lead people from poverty to riches, from condemnation to justification, from weakness to strength and from slavery to freedom.
Does grace also bless you through faith? Let me take you through some priceless questions that could open your potentials up for great exploits.

### a) Are you benefitting from the grace of God?

*But by the grace of God I am what I am: and his grace which was bestowed upon me was not in vain; but I laboured more abundantly than they all: yet not I, but the grace of God which was with me. 1 Cor. 15:10*

By the grace of God, I am what I am!
Are you also aware that there is sufficient grace available for you in Christ? Grace is the source of all extraordinary kingdom exploits.
In the KOG, it is never by power or might but by the spirit of the Lord. That is why all sons of God can lay claim to victory at all time.
The grace of God is ever sufficient to those who will amass sufficient faith to tap into it. Many obtain God's grace in vain believing they need not do any good work anymore. Apostle Paul told us how to make grace effective. He laboured more. Grace has raised us into all good works.
Faith without work is fake. Grace not used to accomplish good work is in vain. We need to learn to labour more so that God's grace can be used

to accomplish more by our service. Moses lost prematurely to pride and haste. He had to spend 40 years to learn those missing skills before God reinstalled his leadership role over his people.

### b) Are you maximizing God's grace?

*For we are God's handiwork, created in Christ Jesus to do good works, which God prepared in advance for us to do. Eph.2:10.*

His grace which was bestowed upon me was not in vain!
Are you maximizing God's grace upon your life or is it in vain?
Apostle Paul showed us how to maximize the grace of God by continuing to labour in grace. The grace of God upon our lives is not meant to be taken in vain. It is meant to labour for the glory of God. Using the grace of God upon our lives to do the good works God purposed our existence to achieve is the way to maximize the grace.
It's time to position yourself for proper exploits by Grace.
I once read a touching story about a man whose lifelong dream was to board a cruise ship and sail the Mediterranean Sea.
He dreamed of walking the streets of Rome, Athens, and Istanbul.
He saved every penny until he had enough for his passage.
Since money was tight, he brought an extra suitcase filled with cans of beans, boxes of crackers, and bags of powdered lemonade, and that is what he lived on every day.
He would have loved to take part in the many activities offered on the ship—working out in the gym, playing miniature golf, and swimming in the pool. He envied those who went to movies, shows, and cultural presentations. And, oh, how he yearned for only a taste of the amazing food he saw on the ship—every meal appeared to be a feast!
But the man wanted to spend so very little money that he didn't participate in any of these. He was able to see the cities he had longed to visit, but for most of the journey, he stayed in his cabin and ate only his humble food.
On the last day of the cruise, a crew member asked him which of the farewell parties he would be attending. It was then that the man learned that not only the farewell party but almost everything on board the cruise ship - the food, the entertainment, all the activities - had been included in the price of his ticket. Too late the man realized that he had been living far beneath his privileges.

In the same way, God's grace is forever sufficient throughout the journey of life. It, however, takes faith to be engraced.

**Is your faith living below the available grace?**

*Jesus looked at them and said, "With man this is impossible, but not with God; all things are possible with God." Mark 10:27*

*"'If you can'?" said Jesus. "Everything is possible for one who believes." Mark 9:23*

Are you labouring more abundantly (like Apostle Paul) in faith?
By this I mean, how far is your faith allowing you access to the Grace?
I am not just talking about the work you do with your faith but about the faith you are using to do the work.
Our faith determines the type and the level of work we can do for the Lord. In the kingdom of God, it is always to you according to your faith. Little faith will pursue little work, and great faith will pursue greater works. Our greatest labour should therefore be in growing our faith.
As far as Christ is concerned, "Our exploits are limited by our faith level!" The grace of the Lord is forever sufficient, but it takes faith to tap into it. We will all face in our lifetime challenges that will demand that we choose, by faith, to live a lifestyle of mediocrity or that of excellence. While an average person will find it easier to make a safe decision to live below his full potential and capacity, with a lot of excuses to support that stand, a faith-filled person can reach towards an excellent realm by operating in the grace of the Lord with faith.
That is what our faith is meant for.
It is meant to obtain what we have not seen (Hebrews 11:1-2).
The race of life is about how much of the ever available and ever sufficient grace of God; each one of us can connect into by our faith.
The good news for every believer is that each of us can liberate and develop excellent potentials within us. You can choose today to release from the deep down within you the unlimited strength, unlimited talents, unlimited peace and love of God.
The human weakness lies not in our lack of potential, but in our "inability" to believe that it exists. It is this lack of faith that makes our mind functions at a fraction of its full effectiveness.
It is by faith we have assurance for things not seen (Heb.11:1).

It is by faith; the elders ahead of us obtain good reports (Heb. 11:2).
It is by faith the Lord created the earth (Heb. 11:3).
It is by faith all the great men in the Bible did exploits (Hebrews 11)
It is by faith you are saved through grace (Eph.2.8-9).
It is by faith we can do greater things (John 14:12-14).
The end time church is purposed to be a body of liberators who will walk in the mighty grace of the Lord, by faith.
The power of the last day Church to reign in victory would be her ability to walk in the grace of the Lord by strong faith!

*In the last days the mountain of the LORD's temple will be established as the highest of the mountains; it will be exalted above the hills, and all nations will stream to it. 3 Many peoples will come and say, "Come, let us go up to the mountain of the LORD, to the temple of the God of Jacob. He will teach us his ways, so that we may walk in his paths." The law will go out from Zion, the word of the LORD from Jerusalem. Isaiah 2:2-3 (Also Micah 4:1-2)*

Grace is simply the most potent force within this dispensation of grace.
All we need to maximize this dispensation is to walk in grace by a high level of faith. We are all called to walk in our full potentials in Christ Jesus.
The potentials available in God's grace are endless.
The exploits available in the Lord remain equally endless.
Nobody is noone's reason for not doing enough exploits.
The only limit we all have is the limit of faith.
The last day church shall be a church of ever increasing grace (Romans 5:10). It shall be a church of greater faith and exploits (John 14:12-14).
As a part of the body, refuse to work by sight but by faith (2 Cor.5:7.)
Without faith, it is impossible to please the Lord (Heb.11:6).
Living outside the faith is regarded as pride (Hab. 2:4).
It is by faith we can rest in the Lord after giving our best.
Sometimes it seems no progress is being made in our race of life, but we need to trust God enough to patiently wait for His right timing.
So tell me what you will set to achieve if you know that you cannot fail?
Set your potential free today by faith as you tap into the limitless grace of the Lord within you.
It is the key to the realm of exploits ever available in the Lord.
The righteous shall live by his faith!

# Other books available from Solomon Osoko:

**FATHERHOOD:**
*Role Modelling God on Earth*

Anyone can be a dad, but it takes a real man to be a father. The influence of a father in a child's development surpasses almost every other influence in this world. Being physically present, however, isn't enough to be a good father.
**Pastor Solomon Osoko says in this book that**: A father's main purpose is to role model God to his children. The scary question is, "If you are not connected to your Heavenly Father, how can you role model Him effectively on earth?"
How can you give a fatherly love that you do not have to your children? A godly father makes having a relationship with God very easy for his children.
Paperback 160 pages / ISBN 978-3-9524512-1-2

**ART OF TRIUMPHANT PRAYER**
*Power of Prevailing Prayer*

You can become all you want to be if all your prayers are answered. That is why it is very important for you to learn and master the triumphant art of prevailing prayers. "After you learn what the disciples learnt from Jesus Christ about prayer, attending Church prayer meeting will become one of the most exciting activities you will cherish in your Christian walk."
Paperback 120 pages / ISBN 978-3-9523844-2-8

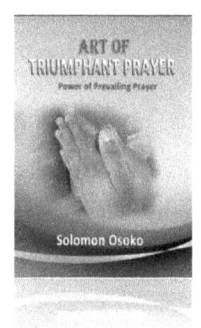

## KINGDOM LEADERSHIP
*Serving Your Generation*

Leadership is an all time important topic to mankind. Many homes, businesses and countries have been ruined for bad leadership. Because leadership problem concerns all men, different institutions have sought different solutions to it. I have over the years watched how business schools take a business approach; and how political schools take a political approach and how Church institutions take a spiritual approach - all to the same issue. The fact, however, is that each of the approaches, though relevant, is as limited as its purview. There is a need for a bigger view. It all starts with changing the way we see and operate leadership.
Paperback 230 pages / ISBN 978-3-9523844-6-6

## FAITHFULNESS IN LEADERSHIP
*Discovering fruitfulness in Faithfulness*

The rise and fall of every organization depend on its leadership.
Smite the shepherd, and the sheep will scatter!
There is no place where this truth is more relevant than in the Church of Christ where it requires the united efforts of a mature congregation and faithful leadership to fulfil God's purpose for His Church. Only rooted and well-established people can bear fruits. Only a faithful leadership, conscious of its responsibility and focused on its calling can take its organization to the next level. We need a culture of faithfulness to reap fruits of our labour. Remember that a big oak tree was once a tiny seed that refused to give up.
Only finishers can be winners.
Paperback 160 pages / ISBN 978-3-9523844-5-9

## GLOWING FROM GLORY TO GLORY
*366 Days Devotional*

Successful walk with the Lord begins with a changed heart, perception and action.
Let Pastor Solomon Osoko lead you on a path of transformation that will take you to a sure destination of joy, perfection and fulfilment. Allow the rich revelations of the word of God in this book to set you aglow from glory to glory. Rise up and shine!
Paperback 370 pages / ISBN 978-3-9523844-9-7

## FELLOWSHIP
*The power link to dominion*

Fellowship with man has always remained a goal of high importance to God from the beginning of creation. For that reason, He made provision for fellowship with every man to be possible.
In this book,
**Pastor Solomon Osoko** boldly affirms that: *"Every form of evil is a departure from the good plan of God and is perpetuated where fellowship with God is dishonored or broken. Every man living outside of fellowship with his Maker simply makes self a defenseless prey for the enemy."*
Paperback 210 pages / ISBN 978-3-9523844-1-1

## FULFILLING YOUR DESTINY
*Living a fulfilled and impactful life*

There is no gain, but chain for a born again Christian that will not use his brain. No matter how born again you are, if you refuse to use your brain, you will fail again. This book will go beyond helping you to locate and fulfil your destiny to establishing your feet on the part of divine fulfilment. You will also discover:
• 4 steps to fulfilling your destiny
• 5 steps to fulfilling a divine purpose
• 6 stages of life
• 12 kingdom keys to keep your heaven open
Paperback 204 pages / ISBN: 978-9523094-0-7

## GOD'S KEY TO SUPERNATURAL BLESSING:
*Sowing a soaring seed.*

This book is particularly dedicated to destroying clouds of ignorance the enemy has been using over the years to cut off the children of the Lord from their heavenly provision and protection thereby subjecting them to sickness, abject poverty, failures and curses.
In this book, you will discover:
• the seven seed principles
• the seven harvest principles
• the impartiality of divine blessing
• all you need to know about tithing
Paperback 192 pages / ISBN: 978-9523094-1-4

## BORN AGAIN TO WIN
*Taking a full step of faith*

This powerful book, spiced with practical faith exercise at the end of every chapter, is sure to help you take the full step of faith into your covenant inheritance in God.
Paperback 120 pages / ISBN 978-3-9523844-0-4


## 40 RELECTIONS ON RELATIONSHIP
*Steps to building great relationship*

What makes a difference between a recluse and a regent? Attitude to relationship!
Building a great relationship is a major responsibility of every decent citizen of the world who aspires to enjoy peace, love and unity in his or her world.
In this book, Ps Solomon Osoko says:
*"There is no second opportunity to make first impression. Mastering good human relationship can easily open you up to your wealthy realms. There is nothing you lack that is not available in other people around you. All you need is the finesse to freely unlock such resources and permit them to enrich your life and that of many others that are connected to you."*
In this book, you will learn reasons, rules and revelations on building a rational relationship.
Paperback 115 pages / ISBN: 978-3-9523844-8-0

You are lovingly invited to FELLOWSHIP with US

@ Christ International Church

**Baden:** Mellingerstrase 26, 5400 Baden, Switzerland
**Bern:** Waldeggstr.37, 3097 Liebefeld – Bern (Koniz), Switzerland
www.cichurch.org
info@cichurch.org

\*\*\*

Also visit our Bible School:

@ Christ International Bible School

For more information:
www.cibsworld.org
info@cibsworld.org

www.ingramcontent.com/pod-product-compliance
Lightning Source LLC
Chambersburg PA
CBHW031320160426
43196CB00007B/592